SURVIVAL ENGLISH

English Through Conversations

Book 2 - Teacher's Manual

SECOND EDITION

Lee Mosteller
San Diego Community College District

Michele Haight
California State University Fresno

Illustrated by Jesse Gonzales

PRENTICE HALL REGENTS

Acquisitions editor: Nancy Leonhardt
Director of Production and Manufacturing: David Riccardi
Editorial production/design manager: Dominick Mosco
Electronic/production supervision, interior design,
  page composition, realia and cover design: Wanda España
Electronic Art: Rolando Corujo and Todd Ware
Production Coordinator: Ray Keating

Illustrations by: Jesse Gonzalez

Printed in the United States of America
12 13 14 15

0-13-016668-5

Contents

Introduction   1

Teaching the Dialogues   2

Literacy Practice with the Worksheets   3

Teaching the Charts   4

Teaching the Reading Passages   5

Teaching the Illustrations   6

Activities and Games   7

Teaching the Sequence Story   8

Vocabulary Practice Through Fill-In Exercises   9

Supplemental Worksheets   9

SURVIVAL ENGLISH BOOK 2 (Page by Page)

Unit 1 – *School*   **12**

Unit 2 – *Clothing*   **19**

Unit 3 – *Food*   **25**

Unit 4 – *Health*   **31**

Unit 5 – *Housing*   **39**

Unit 6 – *Our World*   **45**

Unit 7 – *Transportation*   **50**

Unit 8 – *Emergencies*   **55**

Unit 9 – *Jobs*   **60**

INTRODUCTION

The Teacher's Manual for Survival English Book 2 covers the split editions of books 2a and 2b. Survival English 2 is arranged into nine units: School, Clothing, Food, Health, Housing, Our World, Transportation, Emergencies, and Jobs.

Each unit has a series of dialogues representing survival situations. The dialogues are controlled. Following each dialogue are exercises to reinforce patterns from the dialogues. These include literacy practice with worksheets, charts and other activities. Each unit has multiple illustrations depicting the important vocabulary and the dialogues. Each unit also contains one or more reading passages that are followed by literacy exercises and a review page. For maximum effectiveness, all exercises need to be practiced orally first.

TEACHING THE DIALOGUES

The dialogues are the core of the book and require the most of class time. We have suggested seven steps for teaching the dialogues. For the first five steps, the students keep their books closed.

STEP 1: Have the class listen as you (the teacher) and an aide read the dialogue several times. (If there is no aide, you may read both parts of the dialogue in such a manner that it is clear to the students that two people are talking.) Act out as much as possible and use props to demonstrate the meaning.

STEP 2: Introduce new vocabulary by showing pictures, using props, pantomiming the specific words, and so on. Pronounce the new vocabulary words and have the class repeat them. Write the new words on the board and read them: Have the class read the words. You can review previous language patterns and substitute the new vocabulary with drills.

STEP 3: To begin oral drilling of the new vocabulary in known patterns, introduce a new sentence or phrase from the dialogue. If the sentence is too long for the students, the sentence may be broken into phrases. Have the class repeat. Listen for pronunciation difficulties and review frequently to correct them, striving for the students' understanding, correct pronunciation, and memorization of the dialogue. Have the class repeat the entire dialogue sentence by sentence or phrase by phrase. When applicable, use the illustrations for substitution drills. For example, hold up the picture of downtown and ask, "Where are you going?" The class answers, "I'm going downtown." Practice the A and B parts of the dialogue by dividing the class into two sides. Men can be B, women can be A, and vice versa. Pair practice the dialogue by tables, rows, or any other division in the classroom. When the students are comfortable and successful repeating the dialogue after you, go on to Step 4.

STEP 4: Begin writing the dialogue on the board or uncover the first line on a transparency. Write only one sentence at a time. Read the sentence in the same manner as the class began to speak it. Begin with the new vocabulary that the class has seen at the beginning of the lesson. Read each individual phrase; have the class read it. (Use a pointer to guide their eyes and point out the words.) Next read the entire sentence; have the class read it. Write the next sentence on the board and continue as with the first sentence. Occasionally review earlier sentences. Take time to underline syllables, pronounce words, emphasize the final consonants, and correct other pronunciation difficulties. Continue to write the entire dialogue on the board, one sentence at a time. If the students have begun to commit the dialogue to memory in the third step, they will now reinforce it in their memory and more easily recognize the words.

STEP 5: Keep the dialogue on the board or use the same transparency. Although the students are now going to practice speaking individually without reading the dialogue, they usually feel more comfortable speaking if the dialogue is visible. Encourage them to look at each other while speaking, but let them peek at the board for visual cues if necessary. Help out students if they are struggling, and if a student does not wish to speak in front of the class, respect his or her wish. More learning will occur if the students are comfortable than if they are afraid.

STEP 6: Students now open their books and read the dialogue. Have them underline the new vocabulary words. Give them enough time to make notes or write a translation of the new vocabulary on the page or in their notebooks. Have the whole class read the dialogue chorally a few times before you ask pairs of students to read in the A/B manner. When applicable, encourage them to substitute the vocabulary found at the bottom of many of the dialogues.

STEP 7: Review the dialogue on succeeding days.

LITERACY PRACTICE WITH THE WORKSHEETS

In the student's book, literacy worksheets follow the dialogue. If you notice students having trouble focusing on a particular part of the page, have them use an index card to cover all but the necessary material. Before doing any of the worksheets, drill the patterns orally, using the illustrations you have enlarged to demonstrate vocabulary. Write sample exercises on the board and read them in unison as a class. Then have students read the exercises orally after. Model the correct answer if any student answers incorrectly. Then have the students work in their books. If the students are familiar with most of the words, the literacy exercises will be a great reinforcement. While the class is writing, circulate to help individuals who may be having difficulty. Duplicate the exercise on the board or on an overhead, and when the class has completed their exercises, quickly review the answers by filling in the duplicated copy on the board. Encourage the class to correct their papers from the board. Read the exercise sentence by sentence and have the class repeat. Once again, the class can pair practice the exercise by reading with a partner.

TEACHING THE CHARTS

The student book contains a number of charts, and all of them encourage conversation based on familiar patterns. The charts also help to develop speaking, reading, and organizing skills. In addition, the charts test whether students have mastered vocabulary items and oral patterns, because the students need to construct sentences orally with only a few written cues. The student must remember the vocabulary from the previous units as well as from the current one.

Present the chart by drilling orally with the student books closed. Use the visuals as much as possible to help simulate the chart on the board, or make a copy for the overhead. Simulate the first line of the chart on the board. Ask the questions that are written on the top row of the chart; make sure the class understands the questions. Next call upon a student to answer the questions. Write his/her name on the board. Use abbreviations as short cuts to write down his/her responses because the purpose of the chart is to encourage oral language. After that person has answered all the questions, review them with the class. Then proceed with the next line.

After you have completed the chart line by line, you can ask "who" questions by rephrasing the information on the chart. The class can also write complete sentences about the people interviewed on the chart. If items are compared, the process is much the same. Proceed one line at a time. Ask all the questions in the order they are presented on the chart. Show class how to find information on the chart by looking at the intersection point of the top and the side.

Some charts require the students to query each other for information. Have the students ask the appropriate question and write a short answer in the correct space. Other charts require the student to do some simple calculations before filling in the chart. Pay special attention to these charts and provide the students with ample modeling and guidance in the calculation process as well as with individual attention. If the chart is followed by an exercise, read the questions before and after the class does the activity. (Refer to "Literacy Practice with the Worksheets.") Always review the charts orally in succeeding classes.

TEACHING THE READING PASSAGES

Develop the reading passages as slowly as possible. Do not assume that the students have conquered English, but rather that they are reinforcing their speaking, reading, and writing skills. Make a copy of the illustration on the reading passage page, draw a sketch on the board, or bring in another picture that illustrates the basic idea. Ask leading questions to elicit the story. As the students answer the questions, write the answers on the board, following this example.

Teacher   **Class**

Hold up a visual and ask:

"Who is he?" (Always give the character a name) ...."Faissal"

"What did Faissal bring home?" ...."A letter."

"Faissal brought home a letter.".............................."Faissal bought home a letter."

Write on the board: **"Faissal brought home a letter."**

"Who was the letter from?" ...."His teacher."

"The letter was from his teacher." ...."The letter was from his teacher."

Write on the board: **"The letter was from his teacher."**

"Who did his teacher want to talk to?" ...."His parents."

"His teacher wanted to
  talk to his parents." ...."His teacher wanted to talk to his parents."

Write on the board: **"His teacher wanted to talk to his parents."**
(Continue using visual referent for gender):

"Did he want to have a conference?" ...."Yes, he did."

"He wanted to have a conference."

Read the passage thus far: "Faissal brought home a letter. The letter was from his teacher. His teacher wanted to talk to his parents. He wanted to have a conference." Continue until all the story is on the board. The class has developed an understanding from the questions. Next, have the class read the passage and underline the words they don't know. Have them search for words that you say. Have them circle all the words with endings or all the *he's* that they can find.

After the class has read the entire passage, ask the questions from the worksheets and have the students answer them orally before they reread the entire passage and write the exercise. Next have the students read the passage and the questions or circle the TRUE/FALSE statements. After the class has finished writing the answers, divide the class into two groups to read the questions and answers. Write the questions on the board or use an overhead. Then write the answers, or have the students write them on the board or overhead. Encourage students to correct their work. Encourage them to reread the passage as a review activity.

TEACHING THE ILLUSTRATIONS

Each unit has one or more pages or partial pages of illustrations. Each illustration is numbered. You are encouraged to use the illustrations in creative and innovative ways. The primary purpose, of course, is to teach the vocabulary. You can do this effectively by making transparencies of the visuals and teaching with the overhead projector. By using transparencies you are able to keep the class focused on the same item on the page. Class-size flashcards can be made by projecting the visuals onto paper from the overhead projector and tracing the images onto 8" x 11" flashcards. Use felt pens to add color. With these large visuals you can make substitution drills and continue to reinforce the dialogues, review old vocabulary, play games, develop stories, and so on.

To teach the vocabulary, show the visual and say the word that the picture represents. Add new vocabulary words, but constantly review the words previously introduced. The visuals are numbered so the teacher can ask, "What's number 1?" Class responds. Teacher asks, "What's number 2?" Class responds.

The next activity is to use the vocabulary in the context of the dialogue. Drill the vocabulary in the language pattern by holding up or pointing to the illustrations on the overhead and substituting illustrations. After the class correctly repeats the names of the illustrations, point to or hold up each visual and have the class respond with no prompting. Then develop the dialogue by adding to the language pattern. The class responds according to the picture presented.

You can also practice YES/NO questions by asking for example, "Is it sunny?" Lead the class to say: "Yes, it is." Repeat this drill with many of the visuals. Then add NO questions. Hold up the first illustration again and ask, "Is it cold?" Teacher cues the class to say: "No, it isn't." You may have to cue the students with correct answers frequently throughout the semester. Also point out inflection when asking YES/NO questions. Have the class practice listening and determining whether the sentence is a question or statement. Use the illustrations as much as possible to avoid false interpretations.

The illustrations are also useful for developing literacy. Hold up the illustration and the corresponding flashcard for each word. Read the word, spell the word, count the letters, and underline the syllables. Hand out both illustrations and flashcards to the students and call out a word. The two students who have the flashcard and the visual must stand or hold them up.

Use the illustrations and the flashcards to cue the literacy worksheets. If the worksheet practices YES/NO questions, review them in the manner previously mentioned before the students write in their books. After the students have completed the exercises, read them aloud or ask individuals to read them, or have the class divide into pairs and read the exercises to each other.

Use the illustrations to practice the exercises demonstrated by the charts. Tape the class size illustrations onto the blackboard and draw the lines to simulate the book exercise. Do not proceed with exercises in the book until the class has mastered the vocabulary and is familiar with the oral language patterns.

ACTIVITIES AND GAMES

1. Review the alphabet by dividing the class into teams. You can have have two or more teams depending on how large the blackboard is. Have team members, one at a time, race to the board and write the complete alphabet. The team whose member does it correctly gets the point. Erase the alphabet and start the race again with the next member. Very few students do it perfectly. Those who are too shy should not be forced.

2. Use the page of illustrations found in most units to create games that reinforce vocabulary and language patterns. Make an overhead transparency of the illustrations from the current unit on the blackboard. Review the vocabulary on the overhead. Give two students fly swatters (yes, fly swatters), say one of the vocabulary words on the page, and let the two students race to swat the illustration of the word. Do this for five or six words and then choose other classmates to participate.

3. Tape on the board all the pictures from a unit. Have students from two teams come forward. As you call out the name of a picture, the students race to point to the picture.

4. Divide the class into teams. Give each team a set of flashcards written in a different color so you can tell the teams apart. Tape up pictures and have the teams race to tape all their flashcards below the picture they correspond to.

5. Teach location by placing the visuals around the room. Put the skirt next to the shoes on one wall and the pants next to the socks on another wall. Ask the class, "Where's the skirt?" The students look around the room and respond, "It's next to the pants." This method is especially useful in the units on food, clothing, and transportation.

6. Use the food and clothing units to review money. Have the students place the illustration in front of them so they can write on it. The teacher dictates: "The noodles are $.69." The class finds the picture of the noodles and writes on it "$.69." After you have dictated an amount of money for each picture, test the class by asking, "How much are the noodles?"

7. Students are asked to complete several forms in the book (Registration, Rebate, New Patient, Rental Agreement, etc.). To familiarize students with the large variety of forms used in our culture, introduce and discuss actual forms that students encounter in their daily lives.

8. Whenever possible, encourage students to share their own ideas and experiences in the classroom.

TEACHING THE SEQUENCE STORY

Have students look over all the illustrations. Ask students what they see in the pictures, which are numbered so the class will follow the same sequence. Have students name things they see in the illustrations. Then have them tell the story orally with help from your guiding questions. Using appropriate questions, elicit the story again. Encourage as many students as possible to retell the story from the illustrations.

Following each illustration page is a reading passage based on the illustrations. Practice this in the same way as all the reading passages. The exercises following the passage are for comprehension practice as well as for structure practice. Again, practice orally before the students complete the passage in their books. Then have the class read aloud again. Some questions are open-ended and require the opinions of the class.

VOCABULARY PRACTICE THROUGH FILL-IN EXERCISES

This exercise is a unit review. The sentences used are taken from dialogues and exercises throughout the unit. The illustrations are often a guide to the missing word. Review the illustrations around the exercise first. Orally practice filling in blanks. When students can answer or complete the sentences correctly, let them complete the exercise by writing in the answer. If students forget how to spell any of the vocabulary items, encourage them to look back over the previous dialogues and exercises for the words. Have them read orally when the exercise is completed.

SUPPLEMENTAL WORKSHEETS

At the back of the teacher's manual are black-line masters. Some are to be used after particular pages in the student book, in which case the page number is given on the bottom of the page. If there is no page number, you may use the page where you feel it would best fit the lesson. Many of the worksheets, such as the dictation page on which you dictate lines from the dialogue, may be used again and again. The story page can be used after the sequence stories, or can be used to write stories with the information from the charts.

SURVIVAL ENGLISH (Page by Page)

UNIT 1 – SCHOOL

PAGE 2 — SCHOOL 1

WARM-UP: Preview reading a schedule. Discuss the various kinds of classes offered at an adult school.

DIALOGUE: See "Teaching the Dialogues."

ACTIVITY: Use the class schedule for your site and list other classes the students may take.

PAGE 3

WARM-UP: Preview reading a schedule. To teach the concept of reading down use index cards to cover the other categories. To teach the concept of reading across use the index card to "underline" the line to be read. Ask YES/NO questions to check the students' comprehension of the schedule.

ACTIVITY: See "Literacy Practice with the Worksheets." Substitute other information questions into the exercises. Bring in an actual schedule (bus, school) and use the index cards to assist students in reading it. To check the students' comprehension, ask information questions similar to the ones in the exercises.

PAGE 4 — SCHOOL 2

WARM-UP: Preview introductory phrases. Ask: "Who is he/she?" Students respond: "He/She is _____." Teacher: "Where is he/she from?" Students: "He/She is from _____." Teacher: "It's nice to meet you." Class repeats.

DIALOGUE: Cue the dialogue with names and countries on the board.

Carlos	Hung	Villa
Mexico	Vietnam	Iran

First go over cues orally with students. See "Teaching the Dialogues."

ACTIVITY: When dialogue is mastered, have students introduce one another. Ask students to introduce the person on their left. If a student doesn't know the person, he/she can solicit the information by asking simple information questions: "What is your name?" Where are you from?" Guide the activity and allow students to talk as much as possible.

PAGE 5 — SCHOOL 3

WARM-UP: Preview past tense of **forget**.

DIALOGUE: See "Teaching the Dialogues."

ACTIVITY: Have students fill out the registration cards with their own information. Pair students and have them ask each other information questions, using the head words on the registration cards as cues.

Name: "What is your name?"
Address: "What is your address?"

Teacher can write applicable cues on the board.
See "Literacy Practice with the Worksheets."

PAGE 6

WARM-UP: Preview personal information questions.

ACTIVITY: See "Literacy Practice with the Worksheets."

<u>Note:</u> Questions 8 through 12 require student to fill in information about a friend.

PAGE 7 — SCHOOL 4

WARM-UP: Preview personal pronouns and the verb **think**. *Review the verb* **forget** *and* **won't forget**.

DIALOGUE: See "Teaching the Dialogues." Use illustrations for the substitution drills.

ACTIVITY: See "Literacy Practice with the Worksheets." Have students use illustrations as cues, and complete the worksheet.

PAGE 8 — SCHOOL 5

WARM-UP: Preview school supplies.

DIALOGUE: See "Teaching the Dialogues."

ACTIVITY: Write the names of the school supplies as a dictation or spelling exercise.

PAGE 9 — SCHOOL 6

WARM-UP: Preview indefinite pronouns and the present progressive tense.

DIALOGUE: See "Teaching the Dialogues." Substitute real life situations. "Is anyone standing here?" "Is anyone waiting in line?" and so on.

ACTIVITY: Role play dialogue. Arrange the classroom to fit the situation. Select two students to role play dialogue. Use visual cues such as an eraser, worksheet, and paper within the classroom to cue dialogue.

PAGE 10

*WARM-UP: Review personal pronouns, the verb **think** and the past tense of **forget**.*

ACTIVITY: See "Literacy Practice with the Worksheets."

PAGE 11 — SCHOOL 7

WARM-UP: Preview child care facilities and possible care givers. Discuss the concept of a waiting list. Encourage students to talk about child-care situations in the United States and in their native countries.

DIALOGUE: See "Teaching the Dialogues."

ACTIVITY: Give the students a classroom task to be done weekly or daily, such as writing the date on the board, collecting papers, etc. Assign one or two students to the tasks on the first day. Make a waiting list with the names of all the students on it and post it in a conspicuous place. Have students complete the classroom tasks according to their position on the waiting list. Be sure to cross off those who have already taken their turn. If a student is absent, place his/her name at the bottom of the waiting list. Encourage students to be responsible for their turn. Continue the activity until all students have had a turn.

PAGE 12 — SCHOOL 8

WARM-UP: Preview grades from K through high school. Give the numerical equivalent. Use page 13 as a reference.

DIALOGUE: See "Teaching the Dialogues."

ACTIVITY: Use page 13 as a reference. Have students fill in the worksheet with their own information. Then have students sit in pairs. Use the title words as cues:

NAME, AGE, SCHOOL, GRADE and write them on the blackboard. Students ask each other information questions about their children ("What is the name of your son/daughter?" "How old is he/she?" etc.). See "Literacy Practice with the Worksheets."

PAGE 13

WARM-UP: *Use in conjunction with the dialogue on page 12.*

ACTIVITY: Use in conjunction with the worksheet on page 12. Use the chart as a reference. Ask students about their own educational background. See "Literacy Practice with the Worksheets."

PAGE 14

WARM-UP: *Use page 13 to review grades and numerical equivalents.*

ACTIVITY: Use page 13 as a reference. See "Literacy Practice with the Worksheets."

PAGE 15 — SCHOOL 9

WARM-UP: *Preview the verbs* **be** *and* **have to,** *and the subject pronouns. You can substitute* **need to** *for* **have to.**

DIALOGUE: Encourage students to participate in their children's school activities. Explain that the PTA and other parent groups are open to everyone. See "Teaching the Dialogues." Substitute other phrases of congratulations, such as: Congratulations, That's wonderful, I'm happy to hear that, etc.

ACTIVITY: Complete the sentences using the cues in the boxes.
See "Literacy Practice with the Worksheets."

PAGE 16 — SCHOOL 10

WARM-UP: *Preview the grading system. Use YES /NO questions to test students' comprehension (for example, "Is an A the same as a U?")*

DIALOGUE: See "Teaching the Dialogues."

ACTIVITY: Write A, B, C, D, F on the board vertically. Make flashcards for the other equivalent grades. Hold the flashcard for OK next to the "C." Ask the students: "Is this the same?" See "Literacy Practice with the Worksheets."

PAGE 17 — SCHOOL 11

WARM-UP: Preview school subjects such as reading, spelling, math, behavior. Preview reading a report card. Use page 18 as a reference.

DIALOGUE: See "Teaching the Dialogues."

ACTIVITY: Ask students questions about the grades. "Is the grade in reading O.K?" "What's the best grade?" "What's the lowest grade?" "How many times was the student absent? late?"

PAGE 18

WARM-UP: Review reading a report card. Review the use of index cards to help read a single vertical or horizontal line. Explain the different subjects on the report card.

ACTIVITY: Elicit examples from the class of the subjects on the report card. Write the examples and subjects on the board and match. Have students match the items on the bottom of the page. Refer to this page to answer the questions on page 19. See "Literacy Practice with the Worksheets."

PAGE 19

WARM-UP: Review reading a report card.

ACTIVITY: Use page 18 as a reference to answer the questions. See "Literacy Practice with the Worksheets."

PAGE 20 — SCHOOL 12

WARM-UP: Review personal pronouns and preview possessive pronouns.

DIALOGUE: Have students apply their own information to the dialogue. Cue the dialogue on the blackboard as follows:

Mrs. Tang	Mr. Lee
Lim	Tom
7	2

See "Teaching the Dialogues."

ACTIVITY: See "Literacy Practice with the Worksheets." Substitute son for daughter and practice the sentences. Substitute children for daughter and practice them again.

PAGE 21

WARM-UP: Preview the parts of a letter.

ACTIVITY: Teach recognition of letter parts by listing them on the board and filling them in with the actual data. Draw lines to connect the word "date" with the actual date. Demonstrate alternative ways to write the date and the closing. See "Literacy Practice with the Worksheets."

PAGE 22

WARM-UP: Review the parts of a letter.

ACTIVITY: Assist students in writing a letter to a teacher to excuse an absence. Help students generate the content of the letter orally. Then write what the students generate in the form of a letter on the blackboard. Students can copy the letter in their books or generate their own. See "Literacy Practice with the Worksheets."

PAGE 23

WARM-UP: Review the parts of a letter.

ACTIVITY: Ask students to transfer the underlined information in the letter to the bottom fill-in part of the letter. Have students supply their own son's/daughter's name and their own signature. Assist students in the transference of information. Have students draw a line from the city zoo to the "_____ place" and from "Monday, April 28" to the "_____date." Then have the students transfer the information. See "Literacy Practice with the Worksheets."

PAGE 24

WARM-UP: Have students look at illustrations 1 to 6. Ask them what they see. Encourage all responses. Repeat their responses and model correct sentences. Review the personal pronouns. Review the present and present progressive tenses.

ACTIVITY: See "Teaching the Sequence Story."

PAGE 25

WARM-UP: Review the illustrations on page 24.

ACTIVITY: First read the story to the class, and ask basic comprehension questions. Then, as the class reads the story, have them underline any words they do not know. See "Teaching the Reading Passages."

PAGE 26

WARM-UP: Review the story on page 25 and the illustrations on page 24. Review "wh" and "how" questions.

ACTIVITY: See "Literacy Practice with the Worksheets."

PAGE 27

WARM-UP: Review the Unit 1 dialogues quickly and orally.

ACTIVITY: See "Vocabulary Practice Through Fill-In Exercises."

UNIT 2 – CLOTHING

PAGE 29 — CLOTHING 1

WARM-UP: Preview the names of articles of baby clothing.

DIALOGUE: See "Teaching the Dialogues." Use the illustrations for substitution drills in the dialogue. Students can fill in the name of the person according to their own culture or perhaps the name of a classmate.

ACTIVITY: Bring in actual articles of clothing, utensils, furniture, food, formula and so on, specific to infants. Solicit the names and use of the products from the students. Cue the dialogue by holding up a particular item. Practice the sentences and the questions orally first. See "Literacy Practice with the Worksheets."

PAGE 30 — CLOTHING 2

*WARM-UP: Preview vocabulary used in sewing. Preview or teach **inches, foot,** and **yard.** Bring several yardsticks and measuring tapes to class.*

DIALOGUE: See "Teaching the Dialogues." Use the illustrations as substitutions in the dialogue.

ACTIVITY: On four yardsticks use colored tape or paper to mark the various lengths in the exercises. The teacher can write the colors and equivalents on the blackboard as a reference for students (blue = 1/2 yd., red = 1/4 yd., etc.). Measure various items in the classroom. Ask students to identify the measurements using the color cues as references. Help students with the correct measurements of items that do not fit the color codes. See "Literacy Practice with the Worksheets."

PAGE 31 — CLOTHING 3

WARM-UP: Preview parts of the body and review body measurements.

DIALOGUE: See "Teaching the Dialogues."

ACTIVITY: You may want to bring in tape measures. List men's women's and children's sizes on the board. Note the difference between shoe, sock, and clothing sizes. See "Literacy Practice with the Worksheets."

PAGE 32 — CLOTHING 4

WARM-UP: *Preview the names of articles of clothing. List the commonly visited stores in your area. Bring to class newspaper ads or mailings.*

DIALOGUE: Have students generate the name of a store where they shop to fill in the blank. Explain the word *afford* and the concept *window shopping*. See "Teaching the Dialogues."

ACTIVITY: Reinforce the word *afford* by asking students yes/no questions. Teacher:

> Can you afford to buy a house?
> Can you afford to pay your rent every month?
> Can you afford to take a vacation?

Students answer according to their own information/situation.

PAGE 33 — CLOTHING 5

WARM-UP: *Review the names of articles of clothing.*

DIALOGUE: See "Teaching the Dialogues." Use illustrations as substitutions in the dialogue.

ACTIVITY: As (A), use illustrations as cues for the dialogue and ask students individually, "Can I help you?" Student (B) gives the appropriate response according to the illustration. See "Literacy Practice with the Worksheets."

PAGE 34

WARM-UP: *Preview size abbreviations (S, M, L). Preview types of fabrics (cotton, wool, silk, etc.). Bring real ads to class.*

ACTIVITY: See "Literacy Practice with the Worksheets." Bring in similar ads and go over them with the students. Have the students work in pairs. Have them ask the same information questions as in the exercises, using the new ads as references.

PAGE 35

WARM-UP: *Review the ads and look for the sale prices given in percentages. Be sure the students understand how much the percentages represent.*

ACTIVITY: Read the chart and fill in the blanks. See "Teaching the Charts." Assist the students in computation of 50% OFF (Sale Price).

PAGE 36

WARM-UP: *Preview monetary amounts (such as $10.00, ten dollars). Review the names of articles of clothing. Preview simple subtraction. Preview the percentage chart on page 35.*

ACTIVITY: See "Teaching the Charts." See "Literacy Practice with the Worksheets." Use the illustrations in the chart as substitutions for questions 1 and 2. Assist students to compute the total amount saved. Do subtraction problems on the blackboard, using questions 1 and 2 to get the information from the students.
Ask and the students reply:

    1. What is the regular price of the jogging suits?
    2. What is the sale price of the jogging suits?
    3. How much do you save?
    4. How much do you pay?

PAGE 37 — CLOTHING 6

WARM-UP: *Preview the comparative form of adjectives.*

DIALOGUE: See "Teaching the Dialogues." Use the illustrations as substitutions in the dialogue.

ACTIVITY: See "Literacy Practice with the Worksheets." First practice the opposites of the adjectives. Then list the comparative forms. Ask: "What's the opposite of small?" Class: "Big". Then explain that to compare two items, we add an ending to the word or we use the word *more* before it.

PAGE 38

WARM-UP: *Review the comparative form of adjectives. Review page 37.*

ACTIVITY: See "Literacy Practice with the Worksheets." Use the illustrations to cue the fill-in responses.

PAGE 39 — CLOTHING 7

WARM-UP: *Review the dialogue and worksheet on pages 37 and 38. Practice making comparative statements with **than.***

DIALOGUE: See "Teaching the Dialogues."

ACTIVITY: Use the illustrations to complete the exercises. Bring in actual items such as a purse and a wallet and solicit comparative statements from the students. Students: "The purse is bigger than the wallet. The wallet is smaller than the purse," etc. See "Literacy Practice with the Worksheets." Place some prices on the items and practice *cheaper than* and *more expensive than*.

PAGE 40

WARM-UP: Review percentages. Preview the superlative form of adjectives. Explain that you are now comparing three items.

ACTIVITY: Reinforce difficult vocabulary (such as clearance, stock, entire) and the superlative through repeated repetition and explanation. See "Literacy Practice with the Worksheets."

PAGE 41 — CLOTHING 8

WARM-UP: Review sale vocabulary (such as mark down, clearance, all sales are final, red tag sale) and add vocabulary that the stores in your area might use.

DIALOGUE: The dialogue here is lengthy. If the students have difficulty, break the dialogue into two parts. See "Teaching the Dialogues."

ACTIVITY: See "Literacy Practice with the Worksheets." Demonstrate that prices are sometimes hard to find on tags filled with store codes. Also explain that it's OK to change one's mind at the check-out counter.

PAGE 42

WARM-UP: Have students look at the illustrations in numerical order.

ACTIVITY: See "Teaching the Sequence Story." Ask students to tell the story they see in the illustrations. Model their sentences correctly.

PAGE 43

WARM-UP: Orally review the story on page 42.

ACTIVITY: Read the story to the class and ask basic comprehension questions about it. If the class is able to read the story silently to themselves, allow time for them to do so, and then ask the comprehension questions. See "Teaching the Reading Passages." Note that the questions are in different tenses requiring answers in different tenses. The two-word verb *take back* is split and may be difficult for the class.

PAGE 44

WARM-UP: *Review the story on page 43.*

ACTIVITY: Ask questions orally first. See "Literacy Practice with the Worksheets." Encourage the class to write in complete sentences as they adapt the answers from 1 through 6 to rewrite the story.

PAGE 45

WARM-UP: *Preview vocabulary associated with clothing tags. Preview kinds of fabric. Bring in real articles of clothing. Read the fabric content and laundry tags found in them.*

ACTIVITY: See "Teaching the Reading Passages." Students copy the words following the passage under the illustration of the washer or sink.

PAGE 46

WARM-UP: *Review vocabulary associated with clothing tags. Review kinds of fabric. Review sizes. Look at the tags on real articles of clothing.*

ACTIVITY: Read each label individually and carefully. Reinforce the phrase *made of.* Point to various objects in the room (such as desk, window, eraser) and ask students: "What is it made of?" Have students give an appropriate answer. See "Literacy Practice with the Worksheets."

PAGE 47 — CLOTHING 9

WARM-UP: *Preview the departments in a department or other store. Review the names of clothing and linens. Review* **upstairs** *and* **downstairs.**

DIALOGUE: See "Teaching the Dialogues."

ACTIVITY: Develop new vocabulary by naming an item not listed (sandals, diapers, rings). Have students orally name the department where these items are sold. Match the items and departments in the exercises by drawing a line from one to the other. See "Literacy Practice with the Worksheets."

PAGE 48

WARM-UP: *Review the departments in a department or other store. Preview* **first, second** *and* **third floors,** *prepositions, and adverbs of location.*

ACTIVITY: Have students point to the items as you name them. Ask:: "What is on the first floor? Where is the _____? Where are the _____?". Continue this activity with page 49.

PAGE 49

WARM-UP: Review the departments in a department store or other store. Review floors of stores, prepositions, and adverbs of location. Review page 48.

ACTIVITY: See "Literacy Practice with the Worksheets." Use page 48 as a reference to fill in the exercises.

PAGE 50

WARM-UP: Review the vocabulary demonstrated in the illustrations. Review the Unit 2 dialogues.

ACTIVITY: See "Vocabulary Practice Through Fill-In Exercises."

UNIT 3 – FOOD

PAGE 52 — FOOD 1

WARM-UP: *Preview the names of various food items and the quantities in which they are sold (such as meat/lb., soda/6 pack, cookies/package, etc.).*

DIALOGUE: Discuss vocabulary associated with food ads (on sale, on special). See "Teaching the Dialogues."

ACTIVITY: Bring in actual ads from newspapers and flyers. Ask students information questions about the ads to check their comprehension of the ad such as: "What is on sale?" "How much is it?" "How many can you buy?" Write the abbreviation next to the word it represents.

PAGE 53

WARM-UP: *Preview the sections of a supermarket (for example, produce, meat, dairy) and review the parts of a supermarket (such as aisle, shelf, checkout counter).*

ACTIVITY: See "Teaching the Illustrations." As the students name sections of the supermarket, write them on the board. Add numbers to these words and ask questions such as, " Where do I find bread?" Students respond with the word or the number next to it. Use the questions at the bottom of the page as samples to create more questions.

PAGE 54 — FOOD 2

WARM-UP: *Preview the comparative form of adjectives.*

DIALOGUE: Discuss the concepts of food stamps, WIC coupons, and other ways to pay for food. Discuss the difference between a *produce* and a *grocery store*. See "Teaching the Dialogues."

ACTIVITY: Write the words *cheap, big, small,* and *large* on the board. Tell students when we talk about one item we use this form. When we talk about two items, we add *er* and *than*. You can also review the comparisons from Unit 3. See "Literacy Practice with the Worksheets."

PAGE 55

ACTIVITY: See "Teaching the Reading Passages."

PAGE 56 — FOOD 3

WARM-UP: Preview the superlative form of adjectives and the concepts of **more** and **less**.

DIALOGUE: See "Teaching the Dialogues." Role play situations in which students chose the correct lane.

ACTIVITY: Write pairs of numbers on the board. Guide students in their responses by patterning a correct statement about the numbers, using more or less (" 7——— 45, = 7 is less than 45, 97——— 30 , = 97 is more than 30"). Have the class repeat together orally. Continue the practice asking the class to respond to YES/NO questions ("Is 97 less than 30?"). Finally, solicit the patterned response using *more* and *less than* from individuals. See "Literacy Practice with the Worksheets."

PAGE 57

WARM-UP: Ask students to name the items they know.

ACTIVITY: Cut up the illustrations and make flashcards for the words. Distribute one package of flashcards and illustrations to each pair of students. Working in pairs, both students match visual to flashcard, or one student has the visuals and the other the flashcards. One student shows the other the visual, and the other student finds the matching flashcard or vice versa. See "Teaching the Illustrations."

PAGE 58 — FOOD 4

WARM-UP: Review the comparative form of adjectives and preview **this one** and **that one**.

DIALOGUE: When teaching this dialogue it is helpful to use actual props to convey both the comparative and the concept of *this one/that one*, relating to the proximity of the object. See "Teaching the Dialogues." Use the illustrations as substitutions in the dialogue.

ACTIVITY: Use other comparable objects/illustrations to reinforce both the comparative and *this one/that one*. Pattern the examples. Ask students: "Which one is newer?" Students reply with correct *this one/that one* response. See "Literacy Practice with the Worksheets."

PAGE 59 — FOOD 5

WARM-UP: Review the parts of the supermarket (aisle, shelf, checkout counter). Preview the prepositions of location. Preview negative statements in past tense.

DIALOGUE: See "Teaching the Dialogues."

ACTIVITY: Make the classroom into a store, improvising aisles and shelves. Enlarge the page of illustrations at the beginning of the chapter and place them in various locations around the classroom. Initiate the dialogue by asking as A for a product ("Excuse me, where's the toothpaste?"). Students B answer with directions, patterning the dialogue. Have students as a group repeat the correct directions for each substitution. Have two students take over the roles of A and B and elicit information from each other. Match the opposites at the bottom of the page.

PAGE 60 — FOOD 6

WARM-UP: Preview some of the nutritional vocabulary used with our foods, and encourage students to inquire about words they don't understand on the labels of the products they purchase.

DIALOGUE: Actual products displaying vocabulary presented while teaching the dialogue will help provide substitutions. For example, drill, "Is this low calorie ice cream on sale?" See "Teaching the Dialogues."

ACTIVITY: Bring in products or illustrations that display the vocabulary presented. Write the vocabulary words on the board. Have the students match the product to the vocabulary word. See "Literacy Practice with the Worksheets."

PAGE 61 — FOOD 7

WARM-UP: Review the parts of the store/supermarket (aisle, customer service, etc.).

DIALOGUE: Discuss the concept of rebate and rebate forms. Bring in samples of real rebate forms. See "Teaching the Dialogues."

ACTIVITY Bring in different rebate forms and rebate ads to familiarize students with the concept. Emphasize the difference between coupons and rebates. See "Literacy Practice with the Worksheets." Make copies of other such forms and practice filling them out.

PAGE 62

WARM-UP: Preview the singular and plural forms of the patterned question, using the illustrations as examples. Have the students repeat the examples orally several times before writing.

ACTIVITY: See "Literacy Practice with the Worksheets."

PAGE 63

WARM-UP: *Preview basic addition and its associated vocabulary (add, total, plus, etc.).*

ACTIVITY: See "Literacy Practice with the Worksheets."

PAGE 64 — FOOD 8

WARM-UP: *Read monetary amounts orally ($10.97, ten ninety- seven, ten dollars and ninety- seven cents). Review vocabulary found on coupons (expiration, date, save, limit, etc.).*

DIALOGUE: See "Teaching the Dialogues."

ACTIVITY: Bring in coupons. Teacher asks the same questions as in examples. Students identify how much is saved and what the expiration date is. See "Literacy Practice with the Worksheets."

PAGE 65 — FOOD 9

WARM-UP: *Review monetary amounts. Review reading store receipts using the illustration as an example.*

DIALOGUE: See "Teaching the Dialogues." Point out that the information in the dialogue is taken from the illustration.

ACTIVITY: Help the students identify different parts of a receipt (wt./ price / total). Ask YES/NO questions about the illustration to reinforce students' understanding of a receipt. See "Literacy Practice with the Worksheets."

PAGE 66

WARM-UP: *Review monetary amounts. Review students' experience with reading a receipt by asking YES/NO questions (such as "Are the bananas $4.19/lb.?" "Did the customer buy meat?").*

ACTIVITY: Bring in actual store receipts and follow the same warm-up process. Then ask students the information questions on this page. Repeat this process using different receipts. See "Literacy Practice with the Worksheets."

PAGE 67 — FOOD 10

*WARM-UP: Preview the American tradition of coloring Easter eggs. Explain **dye/color**.*

DIALOGUE See "Teaching the Dialogues." Provide appropriate substitutions such as, "Let's bake some cookies." "Let's cook some rice." Have students generate the needed items in response.

ACTIVITY: See "Literacy Practice with the Worksheets." Name the items needed to dye eggs. This activity is best scheduled before spring break.

PAGE 68

WARM-UP: Preview cooking vocabulary and measurements.

ACTIVITY: Use the illustrations to clarify the written steps for dyeing eggs. Have students repeat the steps several times orally. Bring in needed materials and have the students dye eggs. As the students perform the steps, have them repeat orally what they do. ("Put 1 Tbs. vinegar into a cup."). Cut up the illustrations and mix them up. Have students arrange the illustrations in correct sequence, stating orally which step comes first, second, third, and so on. See "Literacy Practice with the Worksheets."

PAGE 69

WARM-UP: Practice the cooking vocabulary listed on the page.

ACTIVITY: See "Teaching the Illustrations." The illustrations represent; rinse, peel, chop or cut, stir or mix, boil, bake, fry, and pour or add.

PAGE 70 — FOOD 11

WARM-UP: Review cooking vocabulary. Encourage students to talk about food from their native countries. Assist them in explaining their recipes. Emphasize transitional and order words such as first, then, and next.

DIALOGUE: Take role A and go around the classroom asking individual students about his/her favorite food. Assist students with difficult vocabulary emphasizing usage of transitional words: first, then, next. See "Teaching the Dialogues."

ACTIVITY: After the students have sufficient oral practice, assist them to write down their own recipe in the spaces provided on the page. See "Literacy Practice with the Worksheets." Have students ask their classmates about their favorite foods. See "Teaching the Charts."

<u>*Note:*</u> The entire class could put together a cookbook with foods from all the countries represented in the class.

PAGE 71 — FOOD 12

WARM-UP: Teach vocabulary for outdated products. Preview ordinal numbers used with dates.

DIALOGUE: See "Teaching the Dialogues." Use the illustrations as substitutions in the dialogue.

ACTIVITY: After sufficient oral practice with the new vocabulary, enlarge the illustrations and tape them to the board. Make flashcards for the adjectives (sour, stale, spoiled, etc.). Hold a flashcard under the illustration and ask: "Is the milk moldy?" Have the class respond with the correct information, referring to the illustrations and statements for the correct response. See "Literacy Practice with the Worksheets."

PAGE 72

WARM-UP: Review numerical dates (7/8/87, 4/9/88, etc.).

ACTIVITY: Bring in actual products with expiration dates. Repeat the questions shown in the examples, using real products as substitutions. Have the students respond with correct information. See "Literacy Practice with the Worksheets."

PAGE 73

ACTIVITY: Review the unit dialogues. See "Vocabulary Practice Through Fill-In Exercises."

PAGE 75

ACTIVITY: See "Teaching the Visuals." These words are difficult for the students to pronounce. Write the words on the blackboard. Break the words into syllables, underline the syllables, and pronounce each separate syllable, and have the students repeat it. Slowly add syllables together until the students are able to repeat the entire word.

PAGE 76 — HEALTH 1

WARM-UP: Review the adverbs of frequency. Preview vocabulary about the dentist's office and dental care (cavities, fillings, dental floss).

DIALOGUE: Encourage students to discuss their needs, concerns, and possible fears regarding the dentist. See "Teaching the Dialogues."

ACTIVITY: See "Literacy Practice with the Worksheets." Fill in the blanks with the names of illustrations. If possible, discuss what is good for dental health based on the checklist.

PAGE 77 — HEALTH 2

WARM-UP: Preview the vocabulary concerning vision (squinting, blurry, eyechart, etc.).

DIALOGUE: Encourage students to discuss their needs and concerns about their vision. Assist them with difficult vocabulary. See "Teaching the Dialogues."

ACTIVITY: Practice the steps to obtaining prescription eyeglasses.

PAGE 78

*WARM-UP: Review affirmative and negative short answers with **do**.*

ACTIVITY: See "Literacy Practice with the Worksheets."

PAGE 79 — HEALTH 3

WARM-UP: Review affirmative and negative statements. Preview the concept of vitamins and the various forms available as seen in the illustrations.

DIALOGUE: See "Teaching the Dialogues."

ACTIVITY: Fill in the blanks under the pictures. Discuss what is important for good health. Encourage the class to add to this list.

PAGE 80

WARM-UP: *Preview affirmative statements with the modal* **should.**

ACTIVITY: See "Literacy Practice with the Worksheets."

PAGE 81

WARM-UP: *Preview the modal* **should** *in both the affirmative and negative forms.*

ACTIVITY: See "Literacy Practice with the Worksheets."

PAGE 82 — HEALTH 4

WARM-UP: *Preview the days of the week, ordinal numbers, and time. Preview the titles Miss, Mrs., Mr., and Ms.*

DIALOGUE: Discuss what a physical or checkup involves. Encourage students to discuss their experiences at the doctor's office. Ask them if they make doctor's appointments often, and why. See "Teaching the Dialogues."

ACTIVITY: Have the students make their own name tags using their proper title. For example, Mrs. + the husband's last name, Ms. + last name of father, or the way they are named in their countries. Note: first name does not follow a title. Teach the use of the calendar. Dictate different times for certain dates. The class will find the date and write only the time on the date. Check their comprehension by asking afterward, "What time is the appointment on Wednesday, May 15?"

PAGE 83

WARM-UP: *Preview medical vocabulary and pay special attention to the length and difficulty of the words. Break long words into syllables, underline the syllables, and slowly build until students are able to master the pronunciation.*

ACTIVITY: Read sentences several times, using the words in the boxes, so the students learn that a physical is the same as a check-up, etc. See "Literacy Practice with the Worksheets."

PAGE 84

WARM-UP: *Preview the days of the week (and their abbreviations) and time. Preview reading appointment cards.*

ACTIVITY: See "Literacy Practice with the Worksheets." You may be able to get blank appointment cards from your doctor. Try to collect as many different appointment cards as possible.

PAGE 85 — HEALTH 5

WARM-UP: *Preview parts of the body. List on the board the most common childhood diseases, and have the class add to the list. Preview the structure "Have you ever had _____? " Practice affirmative and negative short answers with **have**.*

DIALOGUE: See "Teaching the Dialogues."

ACTIVITY: Take part A and ask individual students the questions in the dialogue. Encourage the class to answer with their own information. Incorporate the vocabulary of the NEW PATIENT FORM on student book page 86 into the dialogue as substitution drills ("Have you ever had liver /bladder/kidney problems?").

PAGE 86

WARM-UP: *Use the "Have you ever been treated for _____?" structure. Review childhood and adult diseases and organs of the body.*

ACTIVITY: Stress the importance of reading forms carefully. The check mark is the same as a YES. Proceed slowly through the form, which students fill out with their own information. See "Literacy Practice with the Worksheets."

PAGE 87

WARM-UP: *Review childhood and adult diseases. Review "Have you ever had _____?" Select three students and insert their names and information into the chart on the blackboard or make on an overhead. Model questions and answers, then demonstrate circling YES or NO in the boxes. Practice "Yes, I have" or "No, I haven't " to answer the questions. Have students ask each other for the information to fill out their charts.*

ACTIVITY: See "Teaching the Charts." Students must refer to the chart to answer the questions.

PAGE 88 — HEALTH 6

WARM-UP: *Ask if any students have allergies and list them on the board. Review the verb* **think.**

DIALOGUE: See "Teaching the Dialogues." Use illustrations as substitutions in the dialogue.

ACTIVITY: Students fill in the blanks using illustrations as cues.

PAGE 89 — HEALTH 7

WARM-UP: *Review short answers with* **do** *and review the verb* **get**. *Practice:* " *I'm allergic to _____. He's allergic to _____. She's allergic to _____, and so on.*

DIALOGUE: See "Teaching the Dialogues." Encourage students to volunteer personal commentary and experience with allergies. Use the illustrations as substitutions in the dialogue.

ACTIVITY: Fill in the blanks with the names of things people are allergic to.

PAGE 90

WARM-UP: *Review the verb* **be** *and the personal pronouns.*

ACTIVITY: See "Literacy Practice with the Worksheets." Complete the sentences.

PAGE 91

WARM-UP: *Review student book page 90.*

ACTIVITY: See "Literacy Practice with the Worksheets."

PAGE 92 — HEALTH 8

WARM-UP: *Review check-up vocabulary such as* **blood pressure, blood sample, urine sample**. *Review affirmative and negative short answers.*

DIALOGUE: The dialogue is lengthy. If students have difficulty, divide the dialogue and teach half at a time. See "Teaching the Dialogues."

ACTIVITY: If possible, bring in a blood pressure cuff, a stethoscope and an odoscope to show the students. Students can role play with one another.

PAGE 93 — HEALTH 9

WARM-UP: *Review the "Have you ever had _____?" structure. Review the days of the week and times of the day.*

DIALOGUE: Discuss prescriptions. Discuss forms of medicine (capsule, tablet, drops, etc.). Encourage the students to talk about their own prescriptions. Break up long sentences and proceed slowly. See "Teaching the Dialogues."

ACTIVITY: See "Literacy Practice with the Worksheets" and page 94. Use the exercises as a reference. Substitute new numbers into the structure "Take it _____ times a day for _____ days."

PAGE 94

WARM-UP: *Review measurements.*

ACTIVITY: Point out that both the whole word and its abbreviation mean the same thing. See "Literacy Practice with the Worksheets." There are three different parts on this page: a match, a rewrite of the underlined letters, and reading and answering the questions.

PAGE 95

WARM-UP: *Review measurements. Review time and measurement abbreviations using page 94 as a reference.*

ACTIVITY: See "Literacy Practice with the Worksheets."

PAGE 96

WARM-UP: *Teach the word **acetaminophen**. You may have this generic medicine in your home. Bring the empty bottle to show its labeling to the class. Review the synonyms **nonaspirin, aspirin-free,** and a **no aspirin product.***

ACTIVITY: The match exercise at the top of the page is included to help the students with the vocabulary in the passage. See "Teaching the Reading Passages." It is important for the students to recognize this somewhat difficult vocabulary and understand it in simplistic terms. Proceed very slowly through the passage so as not to overwhelm the students. Stress the words *warning, dosage,* and *consult.* Look for negative words in the passage such as *not.*

PAGE 97 — HEALTH 10

WARM-UP: *Preview the verb* **hurt.**

DIALOGUE: See "Teaching the Dialogues."

ACTIVITY: Have each students answer questions according to his/her own situation, and ask the same questions of other students in order to complete the chart.

PAGE 98 — HEALTH 11

WARM-UP: *Review and compare* **have** *and* **have to.**

DIALOGUE: See "Teaching the Dialogues."

ACTIVITY: Students fill in exercises using have to + verb and refer to the dialogue for the language pattern.

PAGE 99

WARM-UP: *Preview the parts of a prescription. Review the previous dialogues on medicines.*

ACTIVITY: Draw several boxes on the board to serve as sample prescription forms. Using the illustration as an example, substitute different information on the form. Ask students the same series of questions to test their ability to read a prescription. See "Literacy Practice with the Worksheets."

PAGE 100

WARM-UP: *Review the verb* **have to.** *Review dialogue 11 on book page 98.*

ACTIVITY: Use an overhead or make a sample exercise on the board. Demonstrate how to choose one word from each column to make a complete sentence. See "Literacy Practice with the Worksheets."

PAGE 101 — HEALTH 12

WARM-UP: *Review days of the week, time, and previous dialogues.*

DIALOGUE: Introduce *convenient* as new vocabulary. See "Teaching the Dialogues."

ACTIVITY: Dictate various appointment dates and times. Have students complete the fill-in exercises, (e.g., "It's on Thursday at 8:30.").

PAGE 102 — HEALTH 13

WARM-UP: *Review "Have you ever had _____?" Preview immunizations and an immunization record. Use the illustrations at the beginning of the chapter to reinforce new vocabulary (such as tetanus shot).*

DIALOGUE: See "Teaching the Dialogues." Ask students about their own immunizations and those of their children. Ask where they keep their immunization records, and stress the importance of keeping records for their children and themselves.

ACTIVITY: On the blackboard, draw an immunization record in the form of a chart, or make an overhead of this page. Test students' understanding of the immunization record by asking YES/NO and information questions (for example," Did he have a tetanus shot? When was his first tetanus shot?").

PAGE 103 — HEALTH 14

WARM-UP: *Review body parts and organs. Ask if the students or any of their friends had surgery or an operation of any kind. List the surgeries on the board. Next to them you can also list if they are routine, serious, etc., types of surgery.*

DIALOGUE: Assist students to understand the words *serious* and *routine*. Encourage students to discuss their own operations. Ask them "Was it serious or routine?" Other students continue patterning of the question by asking if it was serious or routine. See "Teaching the Dialogues."

ACTIVITY: Complete the sentences with *routine* or *serious*.

PAGE 104

WARM-UP: *Review future time with **going to** from page 103. Review body parts. Name major organs.*

ACTIVITY: Use the illustration to reinforce students' understanding of body organs. Write the name of the organ on the line in the picture. Complete the sentences. See "Literacy Practice with the Worksheets."

PAGE 105

WARM-UP: *NOTE: Since the correctness of these expressions is in the context of the conversation, it is important to drill each example several times. Encourage students to add new examples.*

STUDENT: My friend lost his job.
TEACHER: I'm sorry to hear that.
STUDENT: My daughter is getting married.
TEACHER: I'm glad to hear that.

ACTIVITY: See "Literacy Practice with the Worksheets."

PAGE 106

WARM-UP: Have students look at the illustrations; ask them what they see. If that is too difficult, ask them to name objects, and pull the story together yourself.

ACTIVITY: See "Teaching the Sequence Story."

PAGE 107

WARM-UP: Review page 106.

ACTIVITY: See "Teaching the Reading Passages." Have students read the statements that follow the story, then decide if they are correct or not. Have students write the correct statements on the following page. If this is done orally first, classmates can correct or help each other.

PAGE 108

WARM-UP: Review page 107.

ACTIVITY: See "Literacy Practice with the Worksheets."

PAGE 109

WARM-UP: Review the vocabulary depicted in the illustrations. Encourage students to refer to previous dialogues and exercises to find the vocabulary they need.

ACTIVITY: See "Teaching Vocabulary Through Fill-In Exercises."

UNIT 5 – HOUSING

PAGE 111

WARM-UP: Preview the rooms of a house.

ACTIVITY: See "Teaching the Visuals." Ask students in what room they would find a particular piece of furniture.

PAGE 112 — HOUSING 1

WARM-UP: Preview **new** and **used.** Review common items able to be purchased used.

DIALOGUE: See "Teaching the Dialogues." Use illustrations on the page in substitution drills in the dialogue.

ACTIVITY: Name the items in the pictures.

PAGE 113 — HOUSING 2

WARM-UP: Review the past tense of **see** and **be.** Review illustrations and previous dialogues.

DIALOGUE: See "Teaching the Dialogues." Use the examples in substitution drills in the dialogue.

ACTIVITY: See "Literacy Practice with the Worksheets."

PAGE 114

WARM-UP: Review **new** and **used.** List the names of well-known discount stores and shopping areas in your neighborhood.

ACTIVITY: See "Literacy Practice with the Worksheets."

PAGE 115 — HOUSING 3

WARM-UP: Preview the names of household items.

DIALOGUE: See "Teaching the Dialogues." Use the illustrations in substitutions in the dialogue.

ACTIVITY: See "Literacy Practice with the Worksheets." Have the students name and spell the items pictured.

PAGE 116 — HOUSING 4

WARM-UP: Review previous dialogues.

DIALOGUE: Write the signs on the board. Explain the difference between vacancy and its opposite, no vacancy. See "Teaching the Dialogues." Ask if anyone is on a waiting list for an apartment, school, job interview, etc.

PAGE 117

WARM-UP: Review the previous dialogue. Preview personal identification terms found on all applications.

ACTIVITY: Fill out the application with the correct information. Answer the questions at the bottom as a self-check list.

PAGE 118

WARM-UP: Review Housing Dialogue 4 on page 116.

ACTIVITY: List the vocabulary words and their abbreviations on the board. Match each abbreviation with its whole word. Read aloud the entire ad for housing , saying the whole word, not the abbreviation. See "Literacy Practice with the Worksheets". Questions 15 through 18 are answered by "A", "B", or "C".

PAGE 119 — HOUSING 5

WARM-UP: Review previous dialogues on housing. Read the new sign.

DIALOGUE: See "Teaching the Dialogues."

ACTIVITY: List things you look for in an apartment. Then demonstrate how to put many of these into questions. Read the nouns in the worksheet, and orally practice the questions. See "Literacy Practice with the Worksheets."

PAGE 120

WARM-UP: Review page 119. Ask students what they see in the picture. Review "Is there _____?" and " Are there _____?"

ACTIVITY: See "Literacy Practice with the Worksheets."

PAGE 121 — HOUSING 6

*WARM-UP: Review the **Is/Are there** construction. Review short answers, both negative and affirmative, with the verb **be**. Preview **move in** and **move out**.*

DIALOGUE: Introduce vocabulary associated with renting (such as utilities, security deposit, rental agreement, etc.). See "Teaching the Dialogues."

ACTIVITY: Read the story and ask comprehension questions about it. Ask the class if anyone is moving or has moved. Review *move in* and *move out*.

PAGE 122

*WARM-UP: Review **don't**. Demonstrate that the circle with a diagonal slash means NO.*

ACTIVITY: Use illustrations to help interpret rules. Assist students with difficult vocabulary. See "Literacy Practice with the Worksheets." Have students volunteer a list of the common tenant rules from their homes.

PAGE 123

*WARM-UP: Preview short answers in both affirmative and negative with **can**.*

ACTIVITY: Have students refer to the illustrations to determine answers, referring to page 122 if they have difficulty answering questions. See "Literacy Practice with the Worksheets."

PAGE 124 — HOUSING 7

WARM-UP: Review past tense, "Did you _____?" Review dates on the calendar.

DIALOGUE: See "Teaching the Dialogues." Explain the importance of keeping receipts.

ACTIVITY: Preview the parts of a receipt. Ask: "What's the date today, tomorrow, Saturday?" Students respond: "It's the_____." Before beginning the exercise, check students' comprehension of reading the receipt by asking YES/NO questions ("Is the rent $500. a month?") Then students read the receipt and answer the questions with information from the form. See "Literacy Practice with the Worksheets."

PAGE 125 — HOUSING 8

*WARM-UP: Review the dialogue on page 124. Explain **late charge.***

DIALOGUE: See "Teaching the Dialogues."

ACTIVITY: Have students supply their own information to answer the questions.

PAGES 126 AND 127

WARM-UP: Review the dialogues on paying rent and due date on pages 124 and 125. Ask if anyone has had a problem paying his/her rent.

ACTIVITY: See "Teaching the Reading Passages." Have students circle the TRUE statements, then copy them on the next page. Also see "Literacy Practice with the Worksheets."

PAGE 128 — HOUSING 9

*WARM-UP: Preview the names of appliances that have a pilot light. Review the present and past tenses of **do**.*

DIALOGUE: See "Teaching the Dialogues." Encourage students to talk of their own experience with pilot lights, leaking gas, and so on. Emphasize the importance of knowing where these are located, and either how to turn them off or to call the manager.

ACTIVITY: Have students answer questions relative to their own situation. See "Literacy Practice with the Worksheets."

PAGE 129 — HOUSING 10

WARM-UP: Preview items related to a power failure (electricity, candles, fuses, etc.). Electricity is a difficult word for students to pronounce. It is helpful to break it into syllables.

DIALOGUE: Encourage students to discuss any similar problems they might have had. List them on the board. Reinforce the importance of saving receipts. See "Teaching the Dialogues."

ACTIVITY: Have students name the items needed in case of a power failure. Their homework assignment will be to get their manager's name and telephone number.

PAGE 130 — HOUSING 11

WARM-UP: Preview and list on the board the items in an apartment that often need to be fixed by the landlord or manager.

DIALOGUE: Teach students to work politely towards a specific time commitment by clarifying "What time _____?" See "Teaching the Dialogues."

ACTIVITY: Assume role B and have students assume role A. Be evasive as students become more assertive with each reiteration of "What time _____?" Have students practice with each other.

PAGE 131 — HOUSING 12

WARM-UP: Review the parts of a letter. Ask students who have moved or are moving if they have written a letter to their landlord.

DIALOGUE: Discuss the need for giving a 30-day notice in writing and the importance of keeping a copy of it. See "Teaching the Dialogues."

ACTIVITY: Have students read the letter and then practice writing a letter with their own information.

PAGE 132

WARM-UP: Preview the various kinds of monthly bills.

ACTIVITY: Have students fill out the YOU section of the chart with their own information. Assist students to total each of the person's bills to complete the chart. This can be done as a class activity. After chart is completed, practice the questions. See "Teaching the Charts" and "Literacy Practice with the Dialogues."

PAGE 133

*WARM-UP: Review the chart on page 132. Review (or add) the vocabulary words, **budget, save, afford**.*

ACTIVITY: Students are required to compute the answers. Assist the students by adding and subtracting figures on the blackboard, eliciting the amounts orally from students (" How much is May's telephone bill?" "$10." "How much is May's food bill?" "$250," etc.) See "Literacy Practice with the Worksheets."

Note: If these worksheets indicate that the class is struggling with basic math, add a basic math skills component to your lessons. Just a few minutes a day can help.

PAGE 134

WARM-UP: *Review the possible monthly bills the students may have. Review the story on page 133.*

ACTIVITY: Have students refer to page 133 to fill in May's information. Then have students fill in their own information. See "Literacy Practice with the Worksheets."

> *Note:* Of course many students will be able to keep a record of their bills and receipts, but some are so overwhelmed by our culture, that they have no idea what to save and what to toss. The shoebox suggestion is an attempt to help those students organize their papers, receipts, bills and so on.

PAGE 135

WARM-UP: *Review the vocabulary illustrated in the visuals around the page. Review the dialogues in this unit.*

ACTIVITY: See "Teaching Vocabulary Through Fill-In Exercises."

UNIT 6 – OUR WORLD

PAGE 137 — OUR WORLD 1

WARM-UP: Preview personal identification questions.

DIALOGUE See "Teaching the Dialogues." Even though the students' command of English may be weak, at this time they are speaking it, for which they should be proud.

ACTIVITY: On the board list the countries and languages. Practice orally: "He's from France. He speaks French. He's French. She's from Mexico. She speaks Spanish. She's Mexican." In the blanks add and include all the nationalities and languages of your students.

PAGE 138

WARM-UP: Review the dialogue on page 137. Make an overhead of this page or use a large world map.

ACTIVITY: Read the paragraph to the students, and allow students to read as well. Substitute the continents in the question, and have students point to them on the paper or on the large map. If you have colored pencils, the class can color the continents so the separations are easier to see. See "Literacy Practice with the Worksheets."

PAGE 139

WARM-UP: Review the dialogue on page 137.

ACTIVITY: Practice the questions as a class first. Then use one student as an example by asking and filling in that student's information. Do not worry about writing complete sentences on the chart. When the chart is completed, have students look back over the chart and write complete sentences. See "Teaching the Charts."

PAGE 140

WARM-UP: Review the exercise on page 138. Have students point to the north, south, east, and west on the map and also in their surroundings.

ACTIVITY: Show that maps usually include the words for north, south, east, and west on them. See "Literacy Practice with the Worksheets."

PAGE 141

WARM-UP: *Review dialogue 1 on page 137.*

ACTIVITY: See "Teaching the Illustrations." Drill with the illustrations and ask for example: "What's number 1?" "Are there mountains in your native country?" "Did you live in the mountains?" "Are there mountains here?"

PAGE 142 — OUR WORLD 2

WARM-UP: *Have students refer to the illustrations on page 141. Have students fill in part B with a YES / NO response and information about their native countries.*

DIALOGUE: See "Teaching the Dialogues."

PAGE 143

WARM-UP: *Review the dialogues on pages 137 and 142, and illustrations page 141. Review "wh" questions.*

ACTIVITY: First practice questions orally. Write the responses on the board and, if necessary, make complete sentences with them . You may want to use only one or two structures, such as "There are rivers." "There are mountains." "There is hot weather." After the class has answered the questions, guide them to write the sentences at the bottom of the page to make a story. Then have the class share their stories. You can compare and chart the countries, weather, capitals and so on.

PAGE 144

WARM-UP: *Since the students are probably all from other countries, you can share this information about the United States, which may be your native country.*

ACTIVITY: See "Teaching the Reading Passages." Show the class how maps will have symbols on them to represent various locations, types of roads, etc. Have the students find the places listed and mark their maps according to the "key."

PAGE 145

WARM-UP: *Review page 144. Bring to class photos or magazine pictures of Washington, D.C., and all the buildings there. The students will appreciate learning about the nation's capital.*

ACTIVITY: See "Teaching the Reading Passages."

PAGE 146 — OUR WORLD 3

WARM-UP: *Review dialogues 1 and 2 on pages 137 and 142. For this activity you may need to provide additional information on your state.*

DIALOGUE: Have the class complete part B of dialogue with their own personal information . When they pair practice the dialogue, they will be practicing true information. See "Teaching the Dialogues."

ACTIVITY: See "Teaching the Reading Passages" and complete the sentences with your state information.

PAGE 147

WARM-UP: *Review page 141 and the dialogues on pages 137, 142, and 146.*

ACTIVITY: The class may be able to complete this individually, but you could also group the class and let them write in groups. Ask if they like the stores and the doctors here. Ask if they miss the flowers and the food in their native countries. You can list all their likes on the board and all the things they miss. Allow lots of time to share the good things here and in their native countries.

PAGE 148 — OUR WORLD 4

WARM-UP: *Preview methods of transportation. Before beginning the dialogue, have two or three students share their stories. It's difficult to understand sequencing in English so, provide guide words like* **first, next, then, after that.**

DIALOGUE: Have the students complete the end of the dialogue with their story and with your guidance. See "Teaching the Dialogues".

ACTIVITY: Refer the students to the pictures for the definition of the verbs. Practice drilling the tenses of the verbs.

PAGE 149 — OUR WORLD 5

WARM-UP: *Review the dialogue on page 148.*

DIALOGUE: Have students circle or mark where they lived before. Then they will be speaking from their own experience. List on the board other places students may have lived .

ACTIVITY: Have the students write the past tense of the verbs listed.

PAGE 150

WARM-UP: Review the dialogues on pages 148 and 149.

ACTIVITY: See "Teaching the Charts." After students have questioned other students and completed the chart, guide them to write complete sentences on the lines provided at the bottom of the page. As always, share the stories.

PAGE 151

WARM-UP: Review the chart on page 150.

ACTIVITY: Draw on the board or make an overhead of page 151. Practice each question with each of the names. See "Literacy Practice with the Worksheets."

PAGE 152

WARM-UP: Review the chart on page 151.

ACTIVITY: First practice the questions at the top of this chart. Then ask questions about May, the example given in the chart. See "Teaching the Charts." Guide students to write the charted information into complete sentences on the bottom of the page.

PAGE 153

WARM-UP: Ask students to look at the pictures and tell you what they see. Point out the number in each picture. Review words to help move the story forward: first, then, next and so on.

ACTIVITY: Have students tell the story in as complete sentences as possible.

PAGES 154 AND 155

WARM-UP: Review the story on page 153.

ACTIVITY: See "Teaching the Sequence Story." The time line is difficult at first, but it's fun. First have students complete the time line by referring to the story. On page 155 students complete the story with the information about themselves, and then transfer the information to the timeline.

PAGE 156

WARM-UP: Repeat the Pledge of Allegiance in front of your class and see if anyone recognizes it.

ACTIVITY: See "Teaching the Reading Passages." The students often want to participate in the Pledge of Allegiance at PTA meetings and with their children at school functions. To become citizens they need to know the Pledge of Allegiance and the facts about the flag.

PAGE 157

WARM-UP: Review page 156.

ACTIVITY: The cloze exercise is based on page 156. Use pictures to share different flags from around the world. Encourage students to draw the flags from their native countries, but be sure you have a reference for those who aren't sure. Have students share their flags.

PAGE 158

ACTIVITY: See "Vocabulary Practice Through Fill-In Exercises." This activity reviews information from the entire Our World unit. Encourage students to look through the unit for the words they need if they're having difficulty.

UNIT 7 – TRANSPORTATION

PAGE 160 — TRANSPORTATION 1

WARM-UP: *Have the class look at the picture. Point to the corner, the light, and the middle of the street.*

DIALOGUE: See "Teaching the Dialogues."

ACTIVITY: Write the words on the blanks and the numbers on the picture for 1. crosswalk, 2. middle of the street, 3. light or signal.

PAGE 161

ACTIVITY: See "Teaching the Illustrations."

PAGE 162 — TRANSPORTATION 2

WARM-UP: *Review the illustrations on page 161. Copy the map on page 162 on the board or use an overhead. Drill and practice directions on the map before looking in the book.*

DIALOGUE: See "Teaching the Dialogues."

ACTIVITY: Use the map to illustrate the dialogue and to practice directions and locations. Have the students complete sentences correctly using information on the maps.

PAGE 163

WARM-UP: *Review the illustrations on page 161. Review page 162.*

ACTIVITY: Have students answer questions about the distance from their homes to these places. See "Literacy Practice with the Worksheets."

PAGE 164 — TRANSPORTATION 3

WARM-UP: *Review Transportation 2. Review left and right by having students point or walk in response to the directions. Teach **block** as from one corner to another corner.*

DIALOGUE: See "Teaching the Dialogues."

ACTIVITY: Have students use their pencils to make a route to the day care center.

PAGE 165 — TRANSPORTATION 4

WARM-UP: Review Transportation 2 and 3. Find a large map of your community. Post the map and highlight the neighboring streets.

DIALOGUE: Everyone will have different directions. Help students complete the directions to their homes. Refer to the map. Encourage more advanced students to write more detail, such as "Go up the hill," "It's the third house," and so on. See "Teaching the Dialogues."

ACTIVITY: Use the exercise for dictation. Read the sentences and fill in the number of blocks and either turn right or turn left.

PAGE 166

WARM-UP: Ask students how they come to school. On the board, list the ways they come. If students don't recognize always, sometimes, usually, and never, refer to the chart on page 167.

ACTIVITY: Have students practice reading the passage, which you have put on the board or overhead. See "Teaching the Reading Passages." Answer questions orally before writing.

PAGE 167

*WARM-UP: Review the concepts represented by **always, usually, sometimes** and **never.***

ACTIVITY: Point out the week days at the top of the chart. Have the students read the chart for the information on when someone comes to school. See "Teaching the Charts."

PAGE 168 — TRANSPORTATION 5

WARM-UP: Ask if any of the students have flown recently or met friends or relatives at an airport. Put up pictures and signs around the room and pretend it is an airport. Copy the sign on the board or make an overhead.

DIALOGUE: See "Teaching the Dialogues." Have students practice giving other students directions based on the signs and props in your room.

ACTIVITY: Help the class to unscramble the three questions at the bottom of the page. Point out that a capitalized word is usually first, and question mark is usually last.

PAGE 169 — TRANSPORTATION 6

WARM-UP: Review the dialogue on page 168.

DIALOGUE: See "Teaching the Dialogues."

ACTIVITY: Luggage and baggage mean the same thing. Have the students alternate these two words in the dialogue.

PAGE 170 — TRANSPORTATION 7

WARM-UP: Review the dialogues on pages 168 and 169. Review YES / NO questions.

DIALOGUE: See "Teaching the Dialogues." Practice the dialogue by using substitution drills with the information in the chart.

ACTIVITY: See "Teaching the Charts."

PAGE 171

WARM-UP: Preview and practice telling time. Review page 170.

ACTIVITY: This activity requires math skills and clock-reading skills. Practice orally with the class first. If they can do it orally, then let them complete the exercise on their own. If it is too difficult, complete it as a class or in groups.

PAGE 172

WARM-UP: Ask students what they remember about coming to the United States. Ask students to tell what they see in the picture.

ACTIVITY: See "Teaching the Sequence Story." Encourage the class to use complete sentences to tell what is happening in the story.

PAGES 173 AND 174

WARM-UP: Review the illustrations on page 172.

ACTIVITY: First, read the passage; then have the students read it as many times as necessary to understand it. Encourage students to read for meaning and not for single words. Ask the basic comprehension questions before the class completes the TRUE / FALSE exercise. After the class has circled "true" or "false," have them write the true sentences on page 174. Then they may complete the written comprehension questions. See "Teaching the Reading Passages" and "Literacy Practice with the Worksheets."

PAGE 175 — TRANSPORTATION 8

WARM-UP: Ask how many students have or want cars. Write the ad on the board, and ask the class if the ad is for a car in good condition.

DIALOGUE: See "Teaching the Dialogues."

PAGE 176

WARM-UP: Review the ad and the dialogue on page 175.

ACTIVITY: Copy one of the ads on the board and ask the questions. Show how the year is abbreviated. Then ask additional questions, such as "How many miles does it have?" or "What's the phone number?" See "Literacy Practice with the Worksheets."

PAGE 177 — TRANSPORTATION 9

WARM-UP: Review the dialogue on page 175.

DIALOGUE: See "Teaching the Dialogues."

ACTIVITY: Have students name the style of the vehicles pictured. Drill the vehicles in the dialogue.

PAGE 178

WARM-UP: Review the dialogues on pages 175 and 177.

ACTIVITY: See "Teaching the Charts." Remember to practice the questions orally before the class writes the answers.

PAGE 179 — TRANSPORTATION 10

*WARM-UP: Review the dialogues on buying a car on pages 175 and 177. Review **will** and **won't**.*

DIALOGUE: See "Teaching the Dialogues."

ACTIVITY: Use **will** or **won't** to answer the questions.

PAGE 180

WARM-UP: *Review the language pattern in the dialogue on page 179. Have students substitute different pronouns in the dialogue.*

ACTIVITY: First demonstrate how to pick one item from each column to make a complete sentence. Then have the students practice orally. The subjects are at the beginning of each sentence. See "Literacy Practice with the Worksheets."

PAGE 181

ACTIVITY: See "Teaching the Illustrations."

PAGE 182

ACTIVITY: See "Vocabulary Practice Through Fill-In Exercises."

UNIT 8 – EMERGENCIES

PAGE 184 — EMERGENCIES 1

*WARM-UP: Bring in a newspaper and share the headlines with the class. Introduce **good news** and **bad news**. Ask the class if anyone has some good news to share.*

DIALOGUE: See "Teaching the Dialogues."

ACTIVITY: Practice substitution drills in the dialogue with the illustrations. Then write these words on the board or dictate them so the class can complete the page.

PAGE 185

WARM-UP: Review the dialogue on page 184.

ACTIVITY: First practice this exercise by dividing the board into two sections: the good news and the bad news. Have the class read the "headlines" and decide if they are good or bad. Have them write on the board and read as a group before completing the exercise in book.

PAGE 186

WARM-UP: Explain to the class what items are necessary to keep in the house in case of emergencies or natural disasters. Practice YES / NO questions.

ACTIVITY: See "Literacy Practice with the Worksheets." 911 may be the emergency phone number in your area. If not, provide the number for the class. Have them write in the numbers as a dictation or listening exercise. Have them get a neighbor's telephone number as a homework assignment.

PAGE 187 — EMERGENCIES 2

WARM-UP: From the class elicit situations in which police are needed and list them on the board.

DIALOGUE: See "Teaching the Dialogues." Have students fill in their most fluent language so the police can call an appropriate translator.

ACTIVITY: Have the students simply answer the questions, or instead write a story about the pictures.

PAGE 188 — EMERGENCIES 3

WARM-UP: Review the dialogue on page 187.

DIALOGUE See "Teaching the Dialogues."

ACTIVITY: Provide phone numbers, or direct the class to find the numbers needed for emergency situations. Discuss or check if you should call the emergency number or the regular number for the five situations listed.

PAGE 189

WARM-UP: Review the dialogue on page 188.

ACTIVITY: See "Literacy Practice Through the Worksheets."

PAGE 190

WARM-UP: Review the two dialogues on pages 187 and 188.

ACTIVITY: Demonstrate the three things to remember in case of an emergency. See "Literacy Practice with the Worksheets."

PAGE 191 — EMERGENCIES 4

WARM-UP: Review the dialogues on pages 187 and 188. Use illustrations or ads of TVs, radios etc.

DIALOGUE: See "Teaching the Dialogues." Use illustrations of appliances for cueing the drill.

ACTIVITY: Match the vocabulary items.

PAGE 192

WARM-UP: Review the dialogue on page 191.

ACTIVITY: Make an overhead or copy the police report on the board. Fill in the form with the information from the dialogue page 191. Then have the students fill in the chart at the bottom of the page by describing the "stolen goods." See "Teaching the Charts."

PAGE 193 — EMERGENCIES 5

WARM-UP: Discuss situations in which you need to call the police. Ask the class what they would do if one of their children didn't come home.

DIALOGUE: See "Teaching the Dialogues".

ACTIVITY: Students accents may make their speech difficult to understand. Use this exercise as a tool to help clarify them. Have students as a class, write a common word that begins with the letter. For example, say "A as in April, B as in ball."

PAGE 194 — EMERGENCIES 6

WARM-UP: Review the dialogue on page 193. This is a continuation.

DIALOGUE: See "Teaching the Dialogues." Have the class write their children's names and practice spelling them. Have the class describe their children and give their ages.

ACTIVITY: Follow the directions on page 193.

PAGES 195 AND 196

WARM-UP: Review the dialogues on pages 188, 191, 193, and 194.

ACTIVITY: Match the vocabulary items. See "Literacy Practice with the Worksheets."

PAGE 197 — EMERGENCIES 7

WARM-UP: Review the dialogues on pages 188, 191, 193, and 194. Practice he/she forms of verbs **have, be,** *and* **do.**

DIALOGUE: See "Teaching the Dialogues."

ACTIVITY: Describe different types of accidents and list them on the board.

PAGE 198 — EMERGENCIES 8

WARM-UP: Review the activity on page 197.

DIALOGUE: See "Teaching the Dialogues."

ACTIVITY: The purpose of this activity is to make students aware that they can help by remembering to record the license plate number. Remind students to stay calm, to get help, and to call the police, (see page 190). You can also make large flashcards of license plate numbers, hold them up for only a few seconds, and have the students write or tell you the numbers they saw.

PAGE 199

WARM-UP: *Review the dialogues and worksheets on accidents on pages 197 and 198.*

ACTIVITY: Students may be able to contribute more ideas than the ones presented here. If so, add them to the list. Review page 190.

PAGE 200

WARM-UP: *Preview the need to have important telephone numbers available.*

ACTIVITY: Bring in phone books for students to use to look up the numbers, or dictate numbers to the class. Remind the class to keep the numbers near their phones.

PAGE 201 — EMERGENCIES 9

WARM-UP: *Review the list of phone numbers on page 200. Have the students find the number of the poison control center. Review personal I.D. questions.*

DIALOGUE: See "Teaching the Dialogues."

ACTIVITY: Explain *conscious* and *unconscious*. The terms are difficult for ESL students to distinguish between.

PAGE 202

WARM-UP: *Review the dialogue on page 201.*

ACTIVITY: Bring to class sample items of poisons usually found in the home, such as medicines, a gasoline can, or alcohol. Have students practice the sentence in the box and drill with the various items. See "Literacy Practice with the Worksheets."

PAGE 203 — EMERGENCIES 10

WARM-UP: *Ask if everyone has a working smoke detector. In many states it's illegal for landlords not to have one in each apartment.*

DIALOGUE: See "Teaching the Dialogues."

ACTIVITY: Have the students complete sentences 1 through 5, using the pattern from the dialogue. "The _____ caught on fire."

PAGE 204

WARM UP: Ask if anyone has been robbed. Ask the class what they would do if they were robbed.

ACTIVITY: See "Teaching the Reading Passages. "Have the class fill in sentences 1 through 4 with *she should*. Encourage additional oral suggestions as to what should be done and write them on the board. Have the class copy from the board or have them try to write their own. Have the class complete number 5 as best they can using the patterned responses as models.

PAGE 205

WARM-UP: Review page 204.

ACTIVITY: See "Literacy Practice with the Worksheets".

PAGE 206

ACTIVITY: See "Teaching the Illustrations." Ask: "What signs say be careful ?" Have the class respond with the numbers of the signs or with the words.

PAGE 207

WARM-UP: Review all the dialogues and worksheets in this unit.

ACTIVITY: See "Vocabulary Practice Through Fill-In Exercises."

UNIT 9 – JOBS

PAGE 209

WARM-UP: *On the board list the jobs the students in the class have or want.*

ACTIVITY: See "Teaching the Illustrations."

PAGE 210 — JOBS 1

WARM-UP: *Review the illustrations on page 209 and YES /NO questions.*

DIALOGUE: See "Teaching the Dialogues."

ACTIVITY: Have the class fill in the blanks with the correct occupation.

PAGE 211

WARM-UP: *Review YES / NO questions.*

ACTIVITY: See "Literacy Practice with the Worksheets."

PAGE 212 — JOBS 2

WARM-UP *Review the dialogue on page 210. Preview **part time** and **full time**.*

DIALOGUE: See "Teaching the Dialogues."

ACTIVITY: See "Teaching the Charts." Have the class interview each other and then write the sentences.

PAGE 213

WARM-UP: *Ask if anyone is looking for a job (the students usually are). Then ask how they are looking. Everyone will agree that jobs are not easy to find here.*

ACTIVITY: See "Teaching the Reading Passages." Have the class read the passage and then circle the true sentences.

PAGE 214 — JOBS 3

WARM-UP: Review the dialogues on pages 210 and 212.

DIALOGUE: See "Teaching the Dialogues."

ACTIVITY: Have the students read each sign and fill in each item. See "Literacy Practice with the Worksheets."

PAGE 215 — JOBS 4

WARM-UP: Review the dialogues on pages 210, 212, and 214.

DIALOGUE: See "Teaching the Dialogues."

PAGE 216

WARM-UP: Preview personal identification questions, such as "What is your name?," "What is your address?," "What is your date of birth?"

ACTIVITY: Help the students complete the job application form with personal information. Explain that if they keep this information available, they won't have to look it up for every application.

PAGE 217 — JOBS 5

WARM-UP: Review the dialogues on pages 210, 212, and 214.

DIALOGUE: See "Teaching the Dialogues."

ACTIVITY: Have the students match the abbreviation with its complete word.

PAGE 218

WARM-UP: Review the abbreviations on page 217.

ACTIVITY: Have the students answer the questions orally before they complete the page in writing. See "Literacy Practice with the Worksheets."

PAGE 219

WARM-UP: *Ask the class if they know anyone here who has job experience from their native countries. Review the vocabulary items that may be new or difficult.*

ACTIVITY: See "Teaching the Reading Passages." Have the students circle TRUE or FALSE after reading the passage.

PAGE 220

WARM-UP: *Tell the class that they are going to help Villa fill out a job application. See "Teaching the Reading Passages." Review items on application. Ask the class: "What is her first name?" and the other questions on the application.*

ACTIVITY: Have the students fill out the application for Villa using the information about Villa in the reading passage.

PAGE 221 — JOBS 6

WARM-UP: *Review the ways to search for a job. Ask if anyone has gone to job training. Ask what classes they had.*

DIALOGUE: See "Teaching the Dialogues."

ACTIVITY: See "Literacy Practice with the Worksheets."

PAGE 222 — JOBS 7

WARM-UP: *Review the dialogues on pages 214, 215, and 217.*

DIALOGUE: See "Teaching the Dialogues."

ACTIVITY: Have the students practice shaking hands and greeting an employer. See "Teaching the Charts."

PAGE 223 — JOBS 8

WARM-UP: *Review the days of the week and telling time. Review the dialogues on pages 214, 215, 217, and 221.*

DIALOGUE: See "Teaching the Dialogues."

ACTIVITY: Have the students look at the illustrations and practice the sentence, "He works the _____ shift." Match the vocabulary items at the bottom of the page.

PAGE 224

WARM-UP: *Review the dialogues on pages 217, 221, 222, and 223.*

ACTIVITY: See "Teaching the Charts." Direct the students to answer questions 1 through 7 after reading the chart.

PAGE 225 — JOBS 9

WARM-UP: *Put a sample paycheck on an overhead transparency or draw one on the board. Ask students whom it is made out to, who it is from, how much it is for, etc.*

DIALOGUE: See "Teaching the Dialogues."

ACTIVITY: Have the students fill in the answers to the questions. See "Literacy Practice with the Worksheets."

PAGE 226

WARM-UP: *Review the transparency of a paycheck. Direct the class to look at the check and find vocabulary items they have learned. Make an overhead or a picture of the check stub.*

ACTIVITY: Point out the information on the check stub. Match items on the left with the definitions on the right.

PAGE 227

WARM-UP: *Review "wh" and "how" questions. Review the parts of a paycheck.*

ACTIVITY: See "Literacy Practice with the Worksheets."

PAGE 228 — JOBS 10

WARM-UP: *Ask if anyone has ever been laid off. Preview* **quit** *and* **fired.**

DIALOGUE: See "Teaching the Dialogues."

ACTIVITY: See " Teaching the Reading Passages." This passage is for the students' information.

PAGE 229 — JOBS 11

WARM-UP: *Review the illustrations on page 209. On the board list the jobs, and next to the jobs, list what the workers did. For example, cook: made soup; gardener: mowed lawns, trimmed trees, planted flowers. List the jobs the students have now, and next to these jobs list their skills.*

DIALOGUE: See "Teaching the Dialogues."

PAGE 230

WARM-UP: *Review the dialogue on page 229.*

ACTIVITY: See "Teaching the Reading Passages" and "Literacy Practice with the Worksheets." At the bottom of this page the students will write their own short story. Have everyone in the class share their stories. They can write on the board or on large sheets of shelf paper.

PAGE 231

WARM-UP: *Have class look at the **before** and **after** pictures. Ask the class what they see. Teach any new vocabulary items.*

ACTIVITY: Have the students read the story. Ask questions about story to judge if the students understand story. See "Teaching the Reading Passages." After class circles TRUE or FALSE, have the students change the responses marked false to make them true.

PAGE 232

WARM-UP: *Review the reading passage on page 231. Review "wh" questions.*

ACTIVITY: Have the class answer the questions orally before they look at the worksheet. Have them pair practice the questions orally before writing their answers in the book. See "Literacy Practice with the Worksheets."

PAGE 233

WARM-UP: *Review these questions orally first. They are based on the dialogues and worksheets in this unit.*

ACTIVITY: See "Literacy Practice with the Worksheets." Use this as a guide for a longer writing. Look at the questions and write the longer answer. Again, encourage students to share their stories with the class.

PAGE 234

WARM-UP: Review all dialogues and worksheets in this unit.

ACTIVITY: See "Vocabulary Practice Through Fill-In Exercises."

Supplementary Worksheets

DICTATION

Listen and write what your teacher says.

1. _____ (page   )

2. _____ (page   )

3. _____ (page   )

4. _____ (page   )

5. _____ (page   )

Now check your answers in the book.

WRITE THE STORY

_____

_____

_____

_____

_____

_____

_____

_____

_____

_____

_____

_____

My name is Hu Tran. My native country is Vietnam. My native language is Chinese. My address in the United States is 2002 South Street, Miami, Florida.

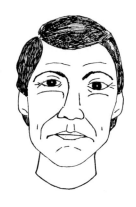

My name is Pablo Lopez. My native country is Mexico. My native language is Spanish. My address in the United States is 6879 Key Street, Yuma, Arizona.

My name is Nao Her. My native country is Laos. My native language is Hmong. My address in the United States is 3485 Tree Street, Houston, Texas.

My name is _____ .
My native language is _____ .
My address in the United States is _____
_____ .

Use this worksheet after page 6 from *Survival English*, Book 2.

1. What country is Hu from?

_____

2. What country is Nao from?

_____

3. What country is Pablo from?

_____

4. What country are you from?

_____

5. What is Pablo's native language?

_____

6. What is Nao's native language?

_____

7. What is your native language?

_____

8. What is Hu's address in the United States?

_____

9. What is Pablo's address in the United States?

_____

10. What is your address in the United States?

_____

I will	I'll
You will	You'll
He will	He'll
She will	She'll
We will	We'll
They will	They'll

1. (I) Tomorrow _____ bring _____ to school.

2. (he) Tomorrow _____ bring _____ to school.

3. (we) Tomorrow _____ bring _____ to school.

4. (they) Tomorrow _____ bring _____ to school.

SOCIAL SECURITY
132-54-6987

5. (you) Tomorrow _____.

6. (she) Tomorrow _____.

7. (my classmate) Tomorrow _____.

Use this worksheet after page 8 from *Survival English*, Book 2.

HOW DID THEY GET THERE?

Answer the questions.

1. How did Hu come to the United States?

   She _____.

2. How did Juan come to the United States?

   He _____.

3. How did Nao come to the United States?

   He _____.

4. How did you come to the United States?

   I _____.

5. How did May come to school yesterday?

   She _____.

6. How did your teacher come to school yesterday?

   _____.

7. How did (your classmate) come to school yesterday?

   _____.

8. How did you come to school yesterday?

   _____.

Complete the sentences with words that tell <u>when.</u>

1. I came to the United States _____.

2. I started English class _____.

3. We take our break in school at _____.

4. School begins at _____.

5. My birthday is _____.

6. My classmate came to the United States in _____.

7. | He | started English class _____.
| She |

8. | His | birthday is _____.
| Her |

9. I eat dinner _____.

10. My classmate eats dinner _____.

11. I met my | husband
| wife
| boyfriend
| girlfriend | _____.

12. My classmate met | his wife
| girlfriend
|
| her husband
| boyfriend | _____.

Use this worksheet after page 154 from *Survival English*, Book 2.

	Yesterday	Usually	Tomorrow
	She _____ a car to school.	She _____ a bus to school.	She _____ to school.
	He _____ to school.	He _____ a car home.	He _____ a bus to New York.
	They _____ a bus to Los Angeles.	They _____ to school.	They _____ a car to New York.

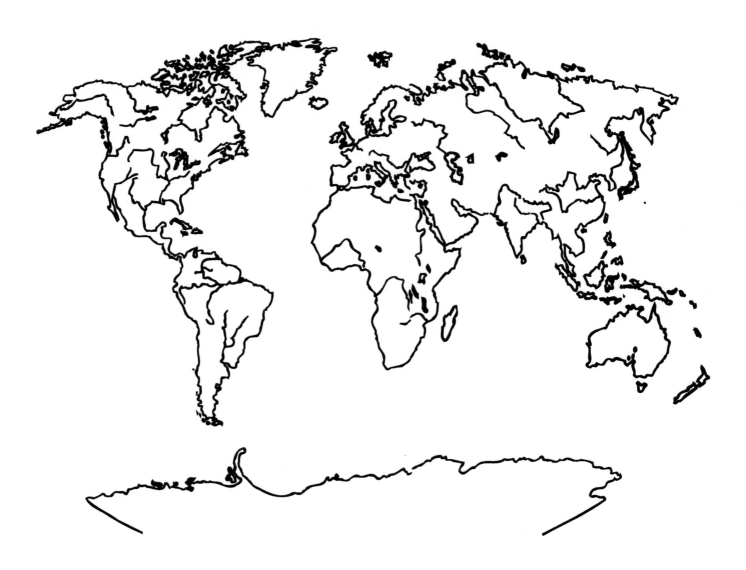

Find you continent.

1. Put a ⚡Z where there are earthquakes.

2. Put a ≋ where there are hurricanes.

3. Put a 🌀 where there are tornados.

4. Put a ⚡ where there are thunderstorms.

Look at the map and answer the questions. If you need help naming the continents, look back into Unit 6.

WORLD WATCH

1. On which continent are there earthquakes?

_____

2. On which continent are there tornadoes?

_____

3. On which continent are there hurricanes?

_____

4. Where are there thunderstorms?

_____

5. Where was the biggest earthquake?

_____

6. Where was the smallest earthquake?

_____

Xay came home from work at 7:00 last night. A stranger was outside his house. Xay didn't know this man. The strange man had a beautiful new TV He wanted to sell the TV for $60. Xay said "No" to the man. He didn't buy the TV Xay thinks the man stole the TV from another house.

Use this worksheet after page 192 from *Survival English*, Book 2.

Xay _____ home from work at 10:00 last night. A stranger _____ outside his house. Xay didn't know him. The stranger _____ a beautiful new T.V. The stranger _____ to sell the TV for $30. Xay said "No." He didn't buy the TV.

1. Who came home from work?

_____

2. When did he come home?

_____

3. Where was the stranger?

_____

4. What was the stranger doing?

_____

5. What did Xay say?

_____

6. Why did Xay say "No"?

_____

7. What should Xay do?

_____

Use this worksheet after page 192 from *Survival English*, Book 2. **79**

Describe your classmates.

Name	Hair	Eyes	Age	Height	Clothes
1.					
2.					
3.					
4.					
5.					
6.					
7.					
8.					
9.					
10.					

MATCH

1. What color? _____
   _____
2. How old? _____
3. How tall? _____
4. What are you wearing? _____

a. Height

b. Age

c. Eyes

d. Clothes

e. Hair

Use this worksheet after page 195 from *Survival English*, Book 2.

Oh, Baby!

Carriage: Trim ¼" off the right side of the page with Scallop and use Fiskars® Press 'n Punch for a vertical row of hearts. Glue a pink (or blue) strip behind the first page to show the lacy effect. Mount the photos on pink and edge the mats with Majestic. Punch enough pink hearts for the letters of the name and trace the baby carriage on page 14 to cut from pink. Write in the birth statistics.

Joshua Jacobs
7 lbs. 2 ounces
21 inches

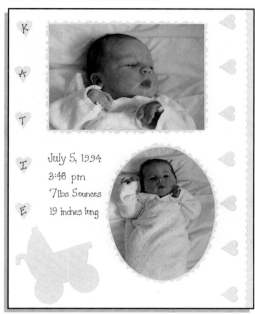

K
A
T
I
E

July 5, 1994
3:48 pm
7 lbs 5 ounces
19 inches long

Our New Arrival

New Arrival: Crop the photos and edge with Scallop; mount on red, yellow or blue and edge again. Trace the heart on page 15 and cut a lavender label with Scallop. Cut rolling green hills with Ripple and use Mini-Pinking to cut two ⅛" wide curving strips for train tracks. Add train and tree stickers, dot a smoke trail winding around the photos, add lettering and finish with small heart stickers to match the paper colors.

Sleepytime: Mount the photos on yellow and edge the mats with Seagull. Cut irregular white shapes with Clouds and use the star shape in Fiskars® Press 'n Punch™ to make yellow stars. Glue all on a blue page and finish with a man-in-the-moon sticker.

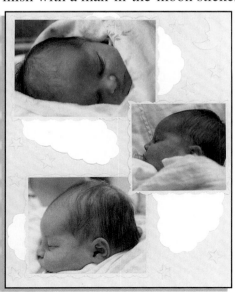

Bathtime: Crop the photos in circles and ovals for bubble shapes and edge with Mini-Scallop. Mount on white, purple and light blue and edge off-center, as shown, with Mini-Scallop. Use Wave to edge the top of a 1"x8" blue strip for the water at the bottom. Decorate with duck and bubble stickers.

First Birthday:

Trace the balloon mouth pattern on page 14 and lay the tracing paper over the photo to draw a round or oval shape capturing the action. Crop the photos with straight scissors, glue on red, blue, yellow or purple paper and edge with Stamp. Trace the "1" and cut from blue paper with Stamp. Cut some plain paper balloons with Stamp. Use straight scissors to cut yellow packages and wrap with red ribbon strips cut with Ripple. Finish with package and confetti stickers.

package pattern

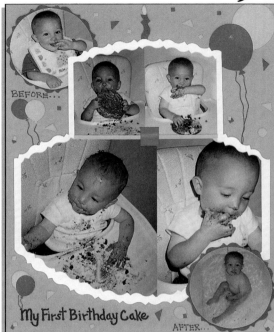

First Birthday Cake:

Arrange large and small photos to fit a two-tiered cake shape. Crop the photos as shown. Leaving the sides straight, edge the tops and bottom with Colonial. Mount on white and edge to match. The candle is a ribbon strip cut with Colonial and the round mats are edged with Colonial. Decorate with balloon and geometric stickers Write "BEFORE…" "AFTER…" and "My First Birthday Cake". Draw balloon strings.

Ballerina Theme Party:

Cut dark pink, lavender, turquoise and lime ribbon strips with Majestic and glue diagonally across a pink page. Edge some of the photos with Colonial before mounting; edge some of the mats with Colonial. Use the heart shape in Fiskars® Press 'n Punch™ to make colored hearts and to punch the corners of one mat. Put different colors of paper behind the punched hearts and glue the hearts as shown.

Balloon Bouquet:

Use the balloon mouth pattern, as described above left, to crop the photos. Glue on pink, purple, teal, red green or yellow paper and edge with Jigsaw. Add some matching plain paper balloons and arrange in a bouquet. Finish with confetti and party hat stickers.

Childhood

First Haircut: Except for the Mini-Scallop on the 1½" square white label, the edging on this album page is done with Dragonback. Draw red stripes on white paper. Edge a photo, mount on the striped paper and edge the mat. Edge oval photos, mount on white and trim with straight scissors, then mount on red and edge again. Trace the barber pole and scissors on page 14. Cut the pole from white and gray paper and draw red stripes. Cut the scissors from silver cardstock. Tie a snip of hair with a red ribbon bow and glue in place. Add lettering in the box.

Bubbles: Use straight scissors to cut close around the people in the photos, then edge the square sides with Victorian. Mount on blue, trimming with straight scissors. Trace the bottle and wand patterns on page 14 and cut from yellow. Cut the threads at the bottle mouth with Mini-Scallop, curves in. Edge the blue label with Pinking and use the star shape in Fiskars® Press 'n Punch™ to decorate the bottle. Add dots and lines with a black pen and finish with iridescent orange circle stickers.

Stacking Blocks: Use a ruler to plan squares, rectangles, triangles and parallelograms on your photos and crop with Stamp. Mount on bright orange, green, yellow, blue or red paper and edge with Stamp. Use Stamp to cut other block shapes to fit the spaces between photos.

Ice Cream: Crop the photos to graduated circles with Ripple, mount on alternating pink and green, then edge with Scallop. Cut long brown triangles with Mini-Pinking and punch pink and green ice cream drips with a teardrop punch. Finish with ice cream stickers.

Everyday Life

Baking: Trace the cookie patterns on page 15 to crop the photos with straight scissors, or trace around your family's favorite cookie cutters. Mount on brown and edge with Mini-Pinking. Glue on cream-colored paper and cut an irregular shape with Wave. Trace the rolling pin on page 14 for a tan label. Add baking stickers and lettering.

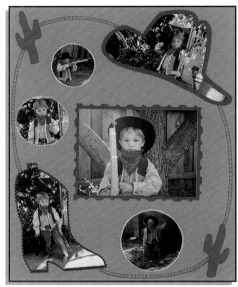

Hey, Dude: Trace the hat and boot on page 14 and use them to crop the photos. Mount the hat on blue; edge with Mini-Pinking. The brown boot is edged with Mini-Scallop. Mount an uncropped photo on brick red and edge with Aztec. Crop photos in circles, mount on cream and edge with Mini-Pinking. Trace the saguaro pattern and cut two from green. Draw a rope to encircle the page.

Vrooom! Crop the photos close around the cars, mount on red, green or yellow paper, then edge with Mini-Pinking. Use Zipper to cut 1" wide curving black strips for roads and mark a center line with a silver pen. Finish with traffic-sign, transportation and tree stickers, cutting ⅛" strips of silver cardstock for signposts.

Sunflowers: Crop photos in circles, mount on light green and edge with Mini-Scallop. Trace the small, medium and large petal patterns on page 14 and cut 8–10 from golden yellow for each flower. Place to overlap behind the photos. Cut dark green stems with Mini-Scallop and light green grass with Mini-Pinking. Use the leaf patterns above to cut light green leaves with straight scissors. Finish with bug stickers.

Family Outings

At the Beach: The water is a 2½" blue strip edged with Wave and the sand is a 2" speckled white strip edged with Fiskars® Rotary Deckle Blade™. The orange sun is cut from the pattern on page 14 and the photo is mounted behind the center hole. The other photos are cropped to show the action, mounted on dark pink, green, lavender and red then edged with (from the top) Jigsaw, Heartbeat, Mini-Pinking and Pinking.

At the Zoo: Edge photos with Stamp and mount on dark green, then edge with Zipper. The light and medium green banana leaves are cut from the pattern on page 14 and the animals are stickers. Notice the lush, jungly effect and sense of depth that result from covering the photos with leaves and animals instead of cropping them.

Bike Riding: Edge the photos with straight scissors or Stamp, mount, then edge with Jigsaw, curves out, to resemble bike chain. Edge three ¾"x⅜" white rectangles with Scallop, curves out, to make clouds. Cut a 1" wide winding black road with Zipper and mark the lines with a silver pen. Finish with flower, bird, bike and tree stickers. Note how the half-trees at the edges give an illusion of more space.

Gone Fishing: Edge the photos with Heartbeat and mount on bright colors. Crop close around a string of fish and mount on green. Trace the fish tail on page 14 and use it when trimming the orange and red mats around the round photos with Mini-Pinking. Punch hearts and glue sideways behind the mats for the fish lips. Place all on blue paper and cut 1" off the top with Seagull. Glue on yellow and decorate with fishing stickers.

The Great Outdoors

Skiing: Crop and mount the photos; edge with Mini-Scallop. Use Fiskars® Rotary Deckle Blade™ on a 1½" wide white strip for the snowdrifts. Place to overlap the feet of the large photo. Finish with white snowflakes and ski stickers.

Canoe Trip: Crop close around the people in a photo and edge the square lower sides with Heartbeat. Edge two photos with Stamp; mount all three on dark green and trim with straight scissors. Crop two photos to ovals, mount and trim with Stamp. Edge a 1¼" dark blue strip with Wave and trace the patterns on page 14 to cut the brown canoe and tan paddle. Punch dark green trees with Fiskars® Press 'n Punch™.

Camping: Use Peaks to cut brown and tan paper in waves and place at the bottom 3¼" of the page for a mountain range. Crop a photo of kids in a tent to the pup-tent pattern on page 15, mount on white and draw stitches around the mat. Tuck behind the front mountains. Edge the other photos with Peaks and mount on cream. Make dark green trees and yellow stars with Fiskars® Press 'n Punch™. The moon, fire and chipmonks are stickers.

Mountains: Crop photos close around the subjects and the dangling hands and arms. Use Peaks to edge 2½" wide dark and light brown strips of paper into rugged mountains and slip under the arms. Mount rectangular photos, trimming the tops with Peaks. Mount again on the other shade of brown, trimming the tops somewhat higher. Punch dark green trees with Fiskars® Press 'n Punch™ to finish.

Summer Days

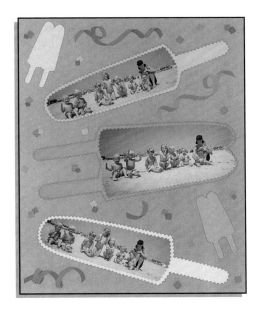

Popsicles: Trace the popsicle pattern on page 14. Crop the photo to the popsicle body and mount on neon orange, red and yellow. Trim the mats to include the popsicle sticks. For the double popsicle, trace the pattern twice and tape to overlap, then make a new pattern. Edge the photos and mats with Stamp. Use the small popsicle pattern to cut pink and hot pink popsicles; finish with confetti stickers.

Watermelon: Crop the photos in half- and quarter-circles and mount on pink. Use Mini-Scallop, with the curves in, to edge. Mount on light or dark green and edge with Scallop, curves out. Edge the curve of a 2¼" pink half-circle and mount on light green to label with the date. Cut a bite out of one tip with Scallop and finish with black seeds made with a teardrop paper punch.

Kites: Use a ruler to draw kite shapes for cropping photos, adjusting the size and angle to fit your subject. Mount on pink, blue and yellow, then edge with Mini-Pinking. Use Ripple to cut rolling hills from a ¾" green strip. Draw kite tails with felt-tipped pens and finish with confetti stickers.

Swimming Pool: The photos are cropped with Dragonback and Mini-Scallop; the mats are trimmed with Mini-Scallop, Scallop and Dragonback. Trace the wave pattern on page 14 to cut three times across the top of a blue sheet; tape on a yellow page and finish with ocean life stickers.

School Days

First Bus Ride: Crop the photos with Zipper, Mini-Scallop or straight scissors, then mount. On the edged photos, trim the black and yellow mats with straight scissors; edge the mats of the straight-cropped photos. Draw a road and cut 1/8" strips of silver cardstock for the signposts on traffic stickers. Label the page (see the letters inside the back cover) and speckle the background with pairs and trios of black dots.

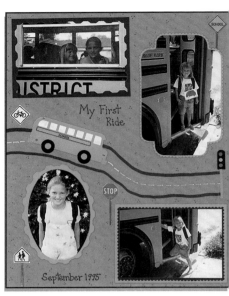

Second Grade: Crop the photos with Stamp, mat on yellow, red, blue and green, and edge with Dragonback. Trace the apple and leaf patterns on page 15 to label the page (see the letters inside the back cover). Finish with school and shape stickers.

Daily Studies: Edge the photos with Jigsaw, mount on blue, yellow, red and green, then edge with Zipper. Trace the crayon patterns on page 14 and use the letters found inside the back cover. Finish with star stickers connected with black dashed and dotted lines.

Field Day: Trim white paper 1/4" in with Pinking and center on a green page. Double-mount the photos on green and yellow or on blue and red, using Mini-Pinking and straight scissors. Trace the prize ribbon pattern on page 15 and cut from blue, red and yellow. Edge the tails with Mini-Pinking. Use Mini-Pinking to cut white circles for red letter stickers and finish with star stickers.

Baseball: Use Peaks to cut a teal diamond and to edge two photos. Mount the photos on red and place to overlap the diamond. Double-mount a team photo, trimming the second yellow mat with Peaks, and place in the center. Crop small photos to circles, mount on white and draw baseball stitches with a pen. Draw similar stitches on white circles made with Fiskars® Press 'n Punch™. Decorate with baseball stickers.

Football: Cut eleven ⅛" white ribbon strips with Mini-Pinking and glue across a green page. Trace the football on page 15 to crop a photo. Tape four ½" white strips to angle out behind the photo and mount on brown. Trim ⅝" away from the photo with Mini-Pinking. Crop other photos and trim the yellow mats with Pinking. Draw yard markers with a white pen. Use Mini-Pinking to edge a 1¾"x1½" yellow label and mount it on lavender. Finish with football stickers and lettering.

Basketball: Trace the backboard and net patterns on page 15 and cut. The pole is a ¾" wide blue strip. Cut a 1" square from the center of a 1½" orange square; glue on the backboard. The orange rim is a ¼" ribbon cut with Dragonback and the mesh of the net is made with teardrop paper punches. Edge a photo with Stamp, mat and trim with Dragonback. Crop other photos in circles, mat on orange and trim with Stamp. Draw bouncing movements and backboard markings with a black pen.

Soccer: This page uses only one Edger: Stamp. Cut a 7½" white circle. Trace the hexagon patterns on page 14. Crop the team photo to the large hexagon and the player photos to the small hexagon. Mount the team photo on black. Cut a curve from one corner to another of a small black hexagon for each of six side shapes. (This is an example of adapting a design to fit the photo being cropped—on a real soccer ball, the center shape would be a pentagon.) Mount a white rectangle on black for a label; finish with soccer stamps and lettering.

Best Friends: Trace the heart patterns on page 15 and enlarge on a copy machine to fit the subject. Crop the photos and double-mount on red, then white (or vice-versa), trimming with Scallop. Use Mini-Scallop to cut and mount a heart-shaped label; letter with a red pen. Use the heart in Fiskars® Press 'n Punch™ to add small hearts.

Easter: Crop the photos in ovals (see inside the front cover) and cut, from pink, purple, green, blue or yellow paper, an oval ⅜" larger all around. Decorate the paper ovals with Ripple ribbon strips and circles, triangle and stars made with Fiskars® Press 'n Punch™. Mount the photos on the decorated ovals and trim with Ripple. Triple-mount a small photo; double-mount a large photo and trim parallel to the first mat for a narrow border. Use the letters inside the back cover to write "Easter" and finish with Easter stickers.

Glorious Fourth: Use Fiskars® Rotary Deckle Blade™ to make seven ⅝" red stripes and cut a 4¼"x3½" blue rectangle. Punch white stars with Fiskars® Press 'n Punch™. Use Stamp and straight scissors to crop and mount the photos to fit the subjects. Trace the star on page 14 for a blue label. Use a white pen to letter and draw stitches on the star.

Headstones: Crop the photos with straight bottoms and curved tops. Edge the bottoms with Peaks. Mount on gray and use Peaks to cut a shadow ¼" away from the curve and right side. Cut additional gray headstones for labels. Finish with spooky stickers.

Weddings

With This Ring . . .

Rings: Mount the photos on green or gold and edge with Majestic. Mount the center photo again on green. The lettering was done by running the white "marble" page through a computer laser printer but hand-lettering with a calligraphy pen is also striking and lovely.

I Thee Wed

Before the Ceremony:
Give pages of wedding photos a dignified look by sticking to simple ovals and rectangles. Choose Edgers with a single pattern or a few similar patterns. Here, crop the photos and mount on navy. Trim with Victorian and place on white "marble" paper.

Two Together: Edge photos with Colonial, mount and edge again, being careful to align the scissors to parallel the photo edge. Double-mount the oval photos with light purple, then plum; edge both mats with Colonial.

Portrait: First edge the white border of the photo with Mini-Scallop, then build a formal frame with three stacked mats of alternating dark and light shades of gray. From the inside, they're trimmed with Victorian, straight scissors and Colonial. Attach to "marble" paper.

Potpourri

Rainy Day Fun:
Crop one photo in a raindrop shape and others in geometric shapes. Mount or double-mount on blue and light blue, trimming with Majestic. Use Mini-Scallop to cut blue paper raindrops sized to fill empty spaces and punch tiny droplets with a teardrop-shaped paper punch.

Carousel: Crop the photos with Mini-Scallop, rounding the corners. Mount on pastel green, lavender and yellow paper, then trim with Ripple. Trace the tent top and flag patterns on page 15; cut from light teal and yellow. Cut a ¼" yellow ribbon strip with Scallop on top and Mini-Scallop on the bottom for a fringe. Decorate with a horse, a pole and musical note stickers.

At the Playground: Crop the photos in a variety of geometric shapes. Cut blue paper to the same size as a rectangular photo; mount ¼" down and right. Trim the exposed edges with Dragonback. Mount the other photos on magenta, yellow, green and red, then trim with Heartbeat, Zipper, Aztec and Jigsaw. Punch circles and triangles with Fiskars® Press 'n Punch™ and add 1cm paper squares. Finish with stickers of children playing.

High-Flyer: Edge the photos with Jigsaw, curves in. Mount on blue or red and trim with the curves out. Mount on red or blue and trim again, curves in. Use Mini-Scallop to cut a waving 1" white strip for a banner. Letter "My First Airplane Ride" in blue and red. Put a chipmonk sticker behind a plane sticker, draw a tow-rope and finish with red and blue star stickers.

And More

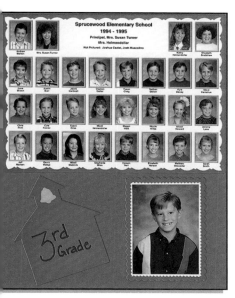

School Pictures: Edge a class photo sheet with Seagull and mount on maroon. Mount an individual photo on white and trim with Mini-Scallop, then mount on maroon and trim with Scallop. Trace the schoolhouse pattern on page 15 and cut from maroon. Draw a bell with metallic gold pen and don't forget to letter the grade!

Autumn: Trace the tree on page 15 and the leaf patterns inside the back cover (or trace leaves from your own trees). Cut a dark brown tree with Stamp and several red, orange and yellow leaves with Mini-Pinking. Crop photos to leaf shapes, mount and edge with Mini-Pinking. Finish with bird and leaf stickers.

Picnic: Cut ⅜" red squares and glue, two rows deep, in a checker pattern around a white page. Use Pinking to cut a green rectangle just big enough to overlap the red checks on all sides. Glue it in the middle. Edge the photos with Mini-Pinking, mount on red and trim with Pinking. Decorate with picnic and chipmonk stickers.

Swim Team: Mount photos on magenta and trim with Scallop or Mini-Scallop, curves in. Mount again on lavender and trim with the same Edger, curve out. Edge aqua paper ¼" in with Clouds for a swimming-pool background; place on a magenta page. Finish with a prize ribbon and splash stickers.

14

bubble bottle and wand, page 3

✿ sun, page 5

star, page 10

✿ patterns © & ™ of *Ellison*™

canoe, page 6

✿ popsicle, page 7

large hexagon, page 9

✿ hat, page 4

canoe paddle, page 6

rolling pin, page 4

small hexagon, page 9

curve for trimming

fish tail, page 5

scissors, page 3

✿ banana leaf, page 5

balloon mouth, page 2

#1, page 2

saguaro, page 4

✿ baby carriage, page 1

barber pole, page 3

✿ popsicle, page 7

✿ wave, page 7

sunflower, page 4

crayons, page 8

✿ boot, page 4

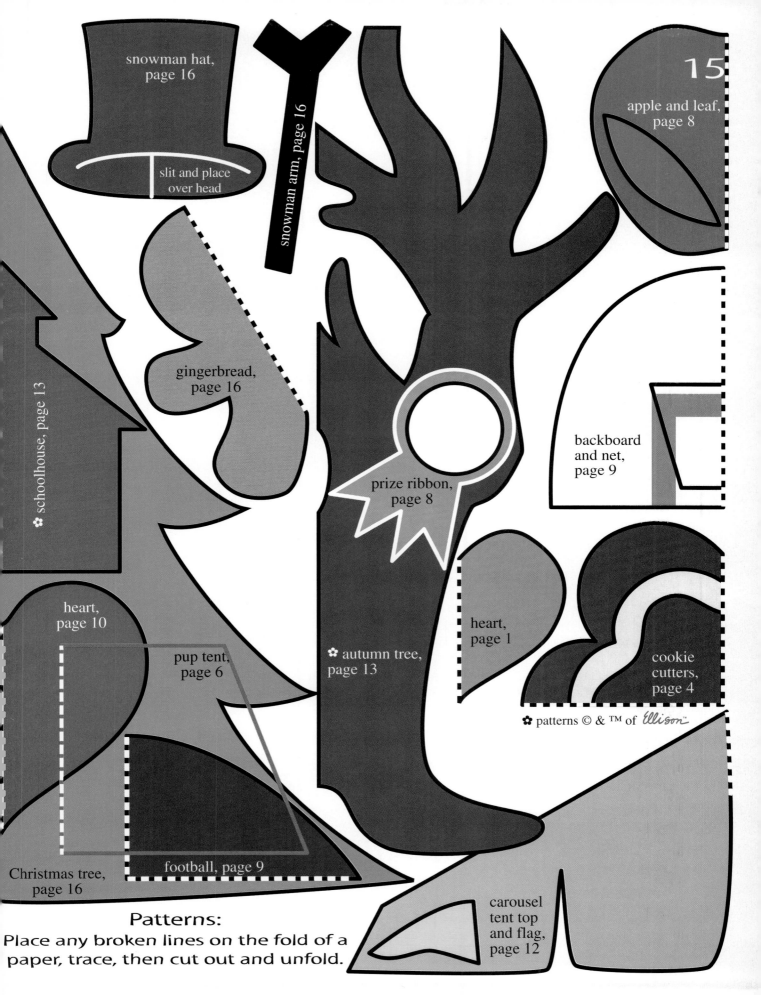

snowman hat,
page 16

slit and place
over head

snowman arm, page 16

15

apple and leaf,
page 8

schoolhouse, page 13

gingerbread,
page 16

prize ribbon,
page 8

backboard
and net,
page 9

heart,
page 10

pup tent,
page 6

❀ autumn tree,
page 13

heart,
page 1

cookie
cutters,
page 4

❀ patterns © & ™ of *Ellison*™

Christmas tree,
page 16

football, page 9

carousel
tent top
and flag,
page 12

Patterns:

Place any broken lines on the fold of a
paper, trace, then cut out and unfold.

Christmas

Christmas Morning: Trace the tree pattern on page 15 and cut from green with Colonial. Use Mini-Pinking to cut a ³⁄₈" brown strip for a trunk. Crop photos to circles or ovals; crop one close around the subject. Mount on lavender, green, orange, blue, pink and yellow; trim closely with Stamp. Make a yellow star with Fiskars® Press 'n Punch™ and cut it in half for the tree top. Finish with stickers of lights, toys and presents.

Snowman: Crop two photos in circles and place the smaller above the larger on white paper. Trace ¼" around them, then draw another circle for the snowman's head. Cut with Ripple and mount the photos on the back. Draw coal eyes and a mouth; use a carrot sticker for the nose. Patterns for the navy hat and brown arms are on page 15. Mount two rectangular photos on white and edge with Clouds. Write "Winter" and scatter trios of dots with a black pen.

Ornaments: Crop the photos in circles with Scallop, Mini-Scallop or straight scissors. Mount on red or green and trim with Clouds. Edge a 1½" red circle with Clouds for a label. Punch yellow hearts with Fiskars® Press 'n Punch™, cut away the bottom points with straight scissors, and cut away the tops with Mini-Pinking. Turn upside-down for ornament hangers. Finish with bow, ribbon and holly stickers. Letter the year.

Gingerbread: Edge photos with Majestic, mount on white and trim with Scallop to look like frosting. Trace the gingerbread man on page 15 and cut with Ripple. Decorate with Scallop and Mini-Scallop ribbon strips on the forehead, wrists and ankles. Draw eyes, mouth and buttons with a white pen.